THE CLONE WARS™

THE WIND RAIDERS OF TALORAAN

DESIGNER **KRYSTAL HENNES**

ASSISTANT EDITOR **FREDDYE LINS**

ASSOCIATE EDITOR **DAVE MARSHALL**

EDITOR **RANDY STRADLEY**

PUBLISHER **MIKE RICHARDSON**

Special thanks to Elaine Mederer, Jann Moorhead, David Anderman, Leland Chee, Sue Rostoni, and Carol Roeder at Lucas Licensing.

STAR WARS: THE CLONE WARS — THE WIND RAIDERS OF TALORAAN

ISBN: 9781848563346

Published by Titan Books, a division of Titan Publishing Group Ltd.
144 Southwark Street, London SE1 0UP

Originally published by Dark Horse Comics.

A CIP catalogue record for this title is available from the British Library.

First edition: June 2009
10 9 8 7 6 5 4 3 2
Printed in China

The events in these stories take place sometime during the Clone Wars.

STAR WARS®

THE CLONE WARS™

THE WIND RAIDERS OF TALORAAN

SCRIPT **JOHN OSTRANDER**   ART **THE FILLBACH BROTHERS**

COLORS **RONDA PATTISON**   LETTERING **MICHAEL HEISLER**

COVER ART **WAYNE LO**

TITAN BOOKS

THIS STORY TAKES PLACE WITHIN THE FIRST YEAR OF THE CLONE WARS.

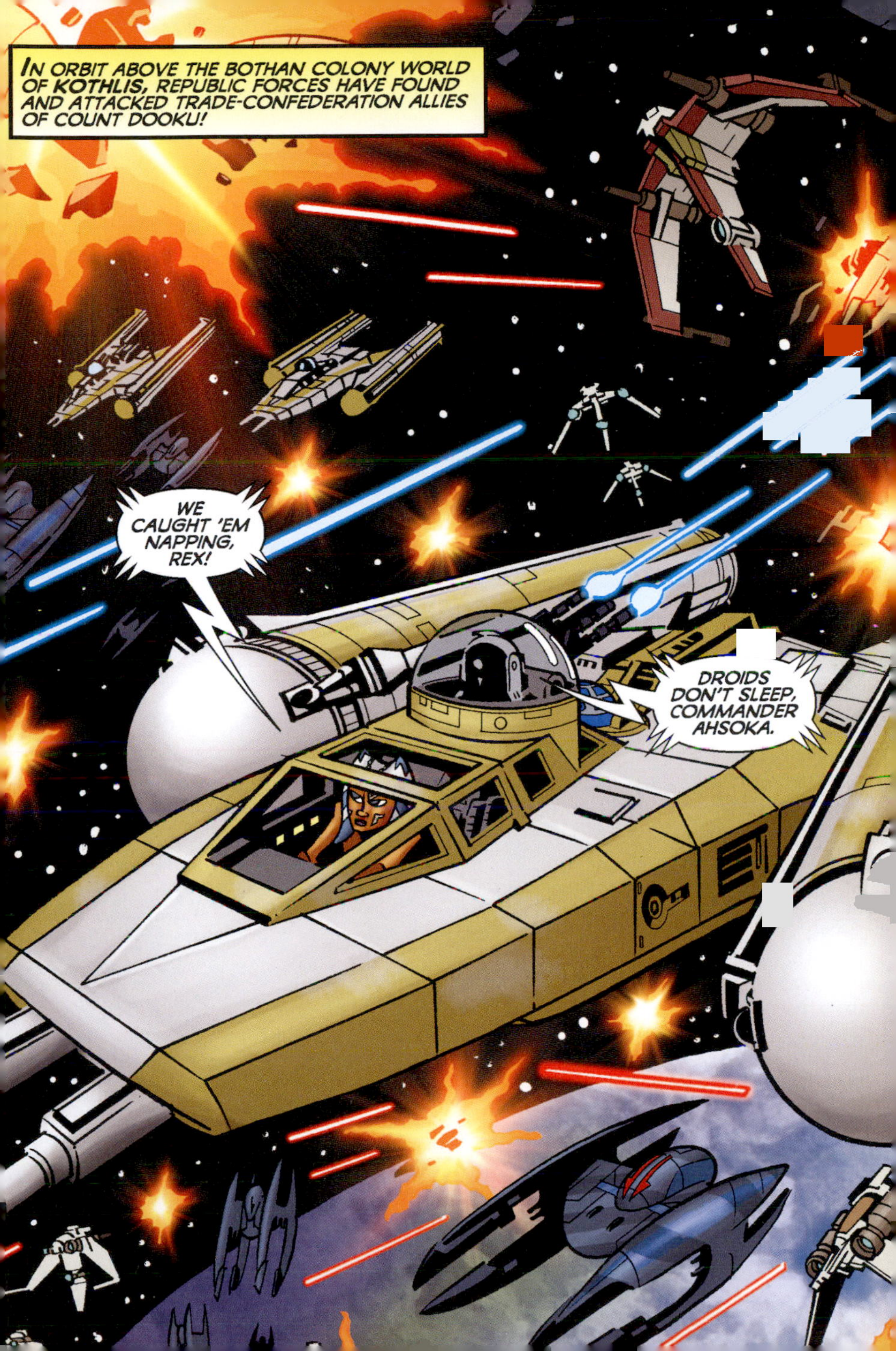
IN ORBIT ABOVE THE BOTHAN COLONY WORLD OF KOTHLIS, REPUBLIC FORCES HAVE FOUND AND ATTACKED TRADE-CONFEDERATION ALLIES OF COUNT DOOKU!
WE CAUGHT 'EM NAPPING, REX!
DROIDS DON'T SLEEP, COMMANDER AHSOKA.

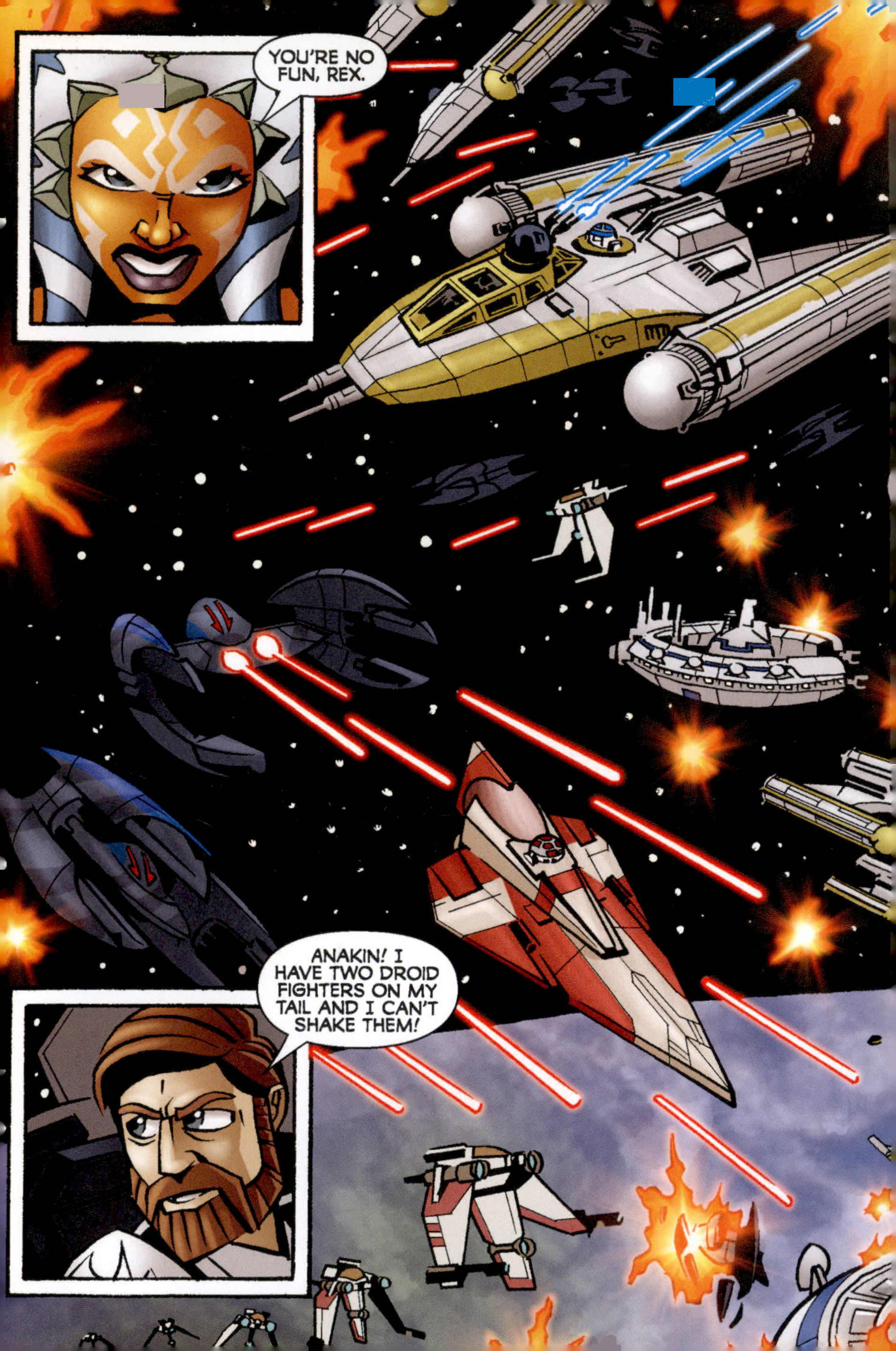
YOU'RE NO FUN, REX.
ANAKIN! I HAVE TWO DROID FIGHTERS ON MY TAIL AND I CAN'T SHAKE THEM!

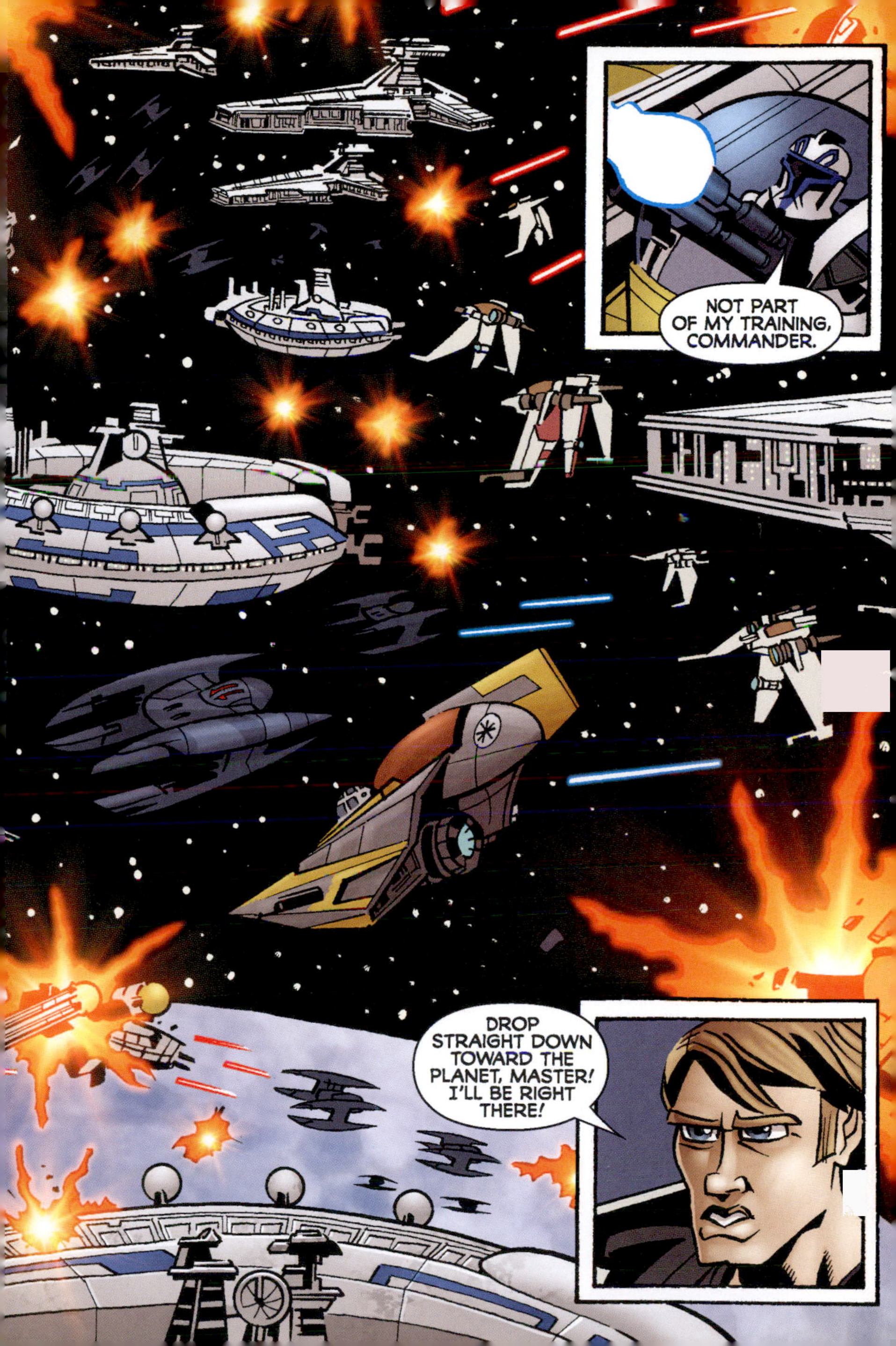
NOT PART OF MY TRAINING, COMMANDER.
DROP STRAIGHT DOWN TOWARD THE PLANET, MASTER! I'LL BE RIGHT THERE!

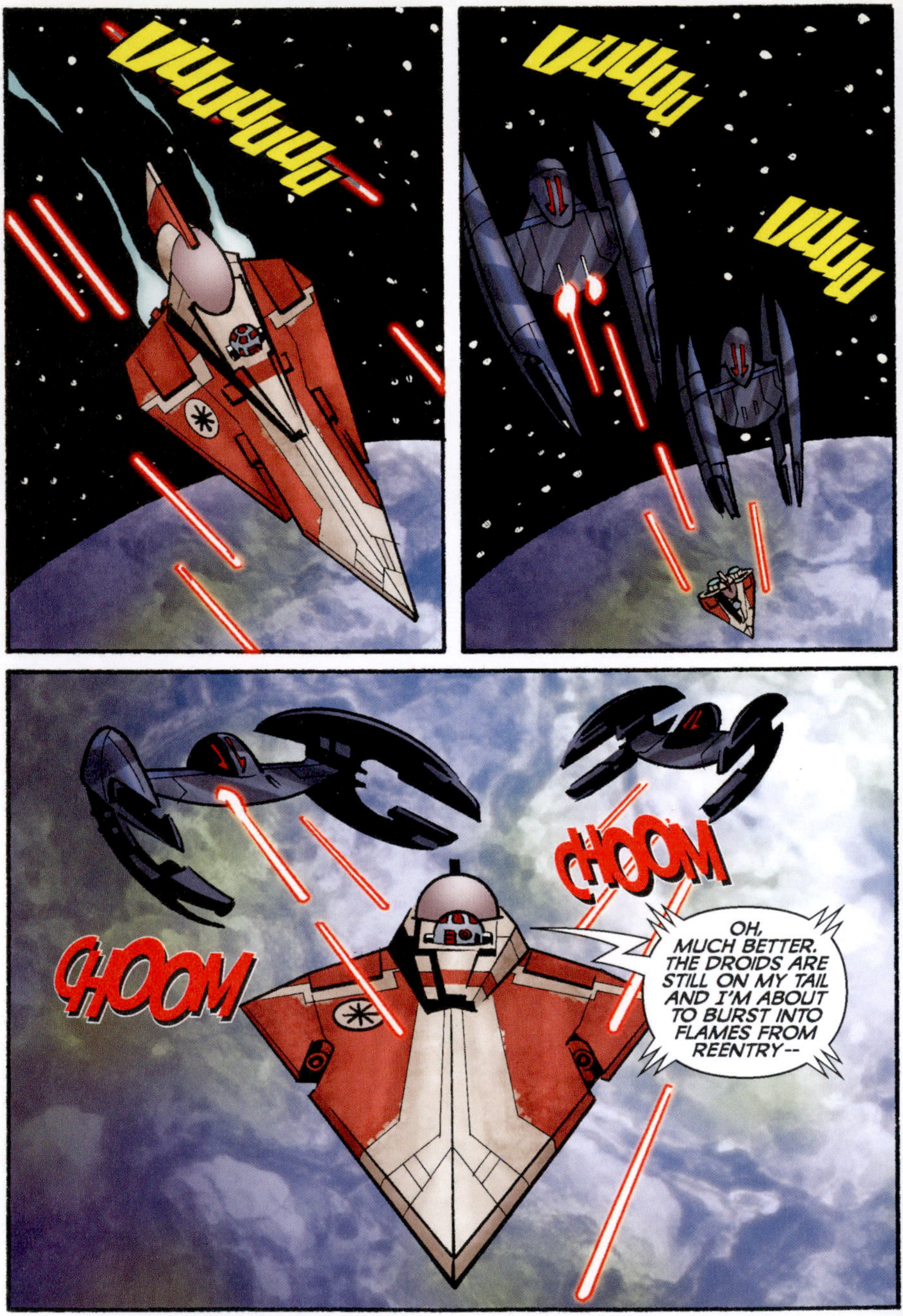
CHOOM
CHOOM
OH, MUCH BETTER. THE DROIDS ARE STILL ON MY TAIL AND I'M ABOUT TO BURST INTO FLAMES FROM REENTRY--

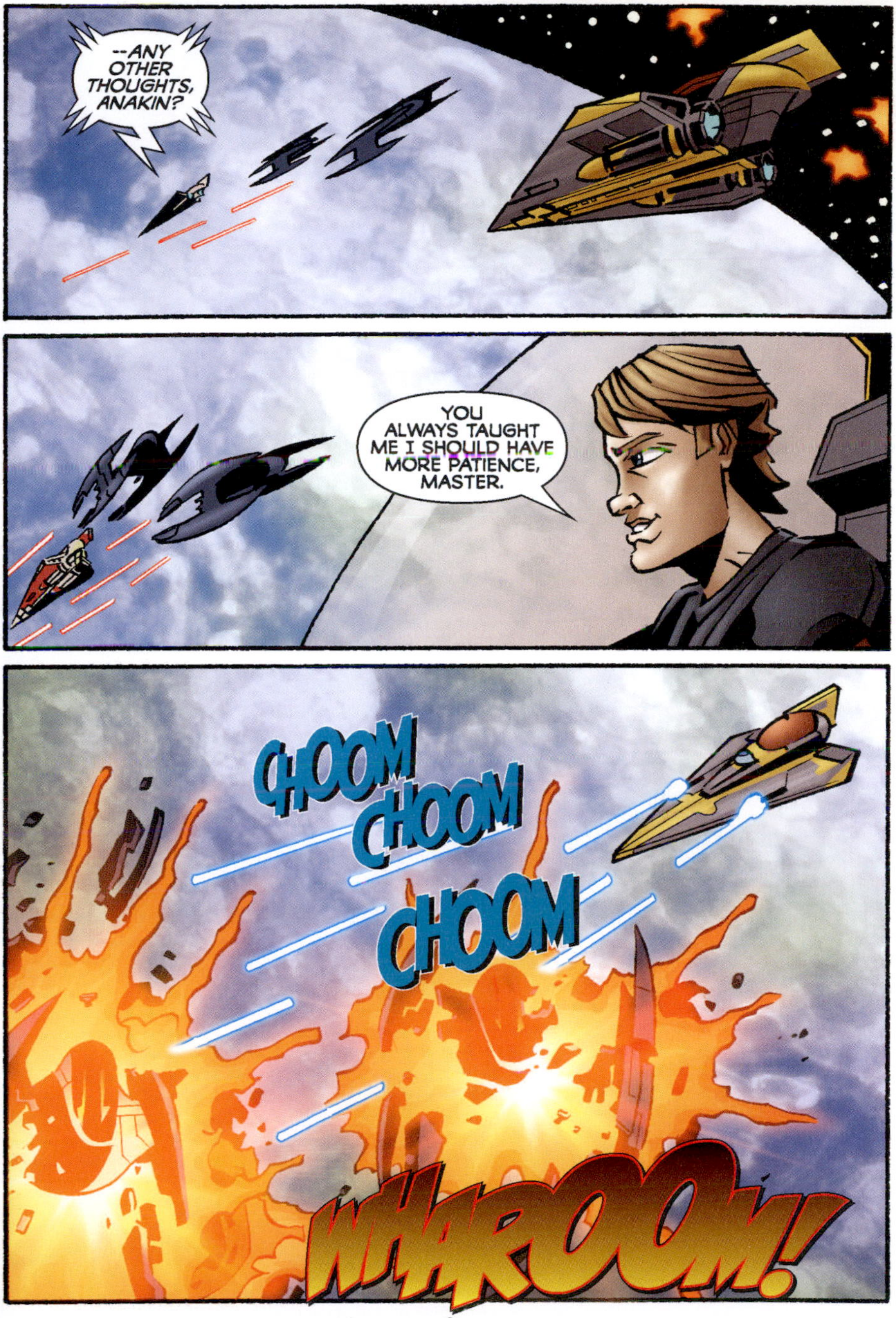
--ANY OTHER THOUGHTS, ANAKIN?
YOU ALWAYS TAUGHT ME I SHOULD HAVE MORE PATIENCE, MASTER.
CHOOM
CHOOM
CHOOM
WHAROOM!

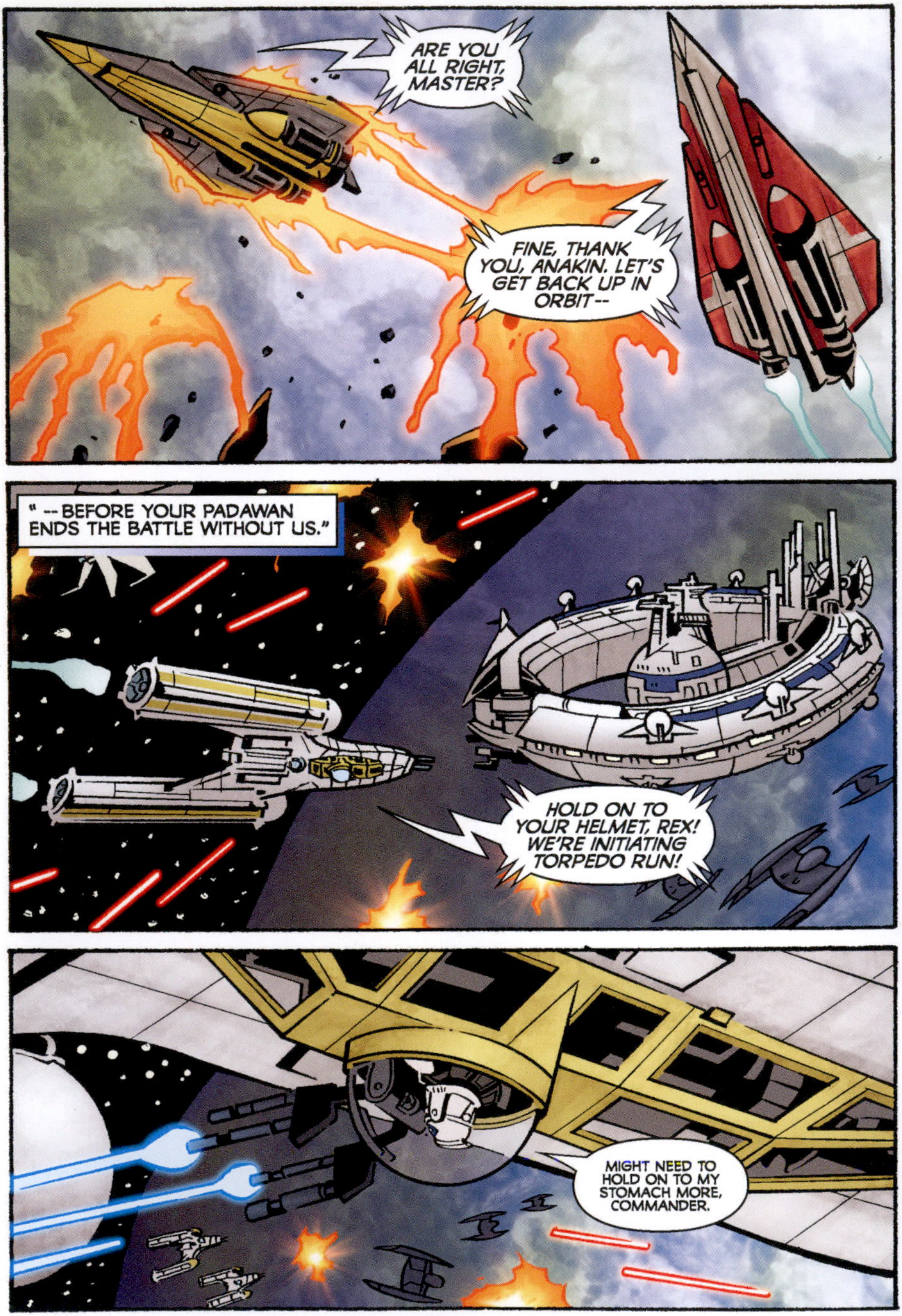
ARE YOU ALL RIGHT, MASTER?
FINE, THANK YOU, ANAKIN. LET'S GET BACK UP IN ORBIT--
" --BEFORE YOUR PADAWAN ENDS THE BATTLE WITHOUT US."
HOLD ON TO YOUR HELMET, REX! WE'RE INITIATING TORPEDO RUN!
MIGHT NEED TO HOLD ON TO MY STOMACH MORE, COMMANDER.

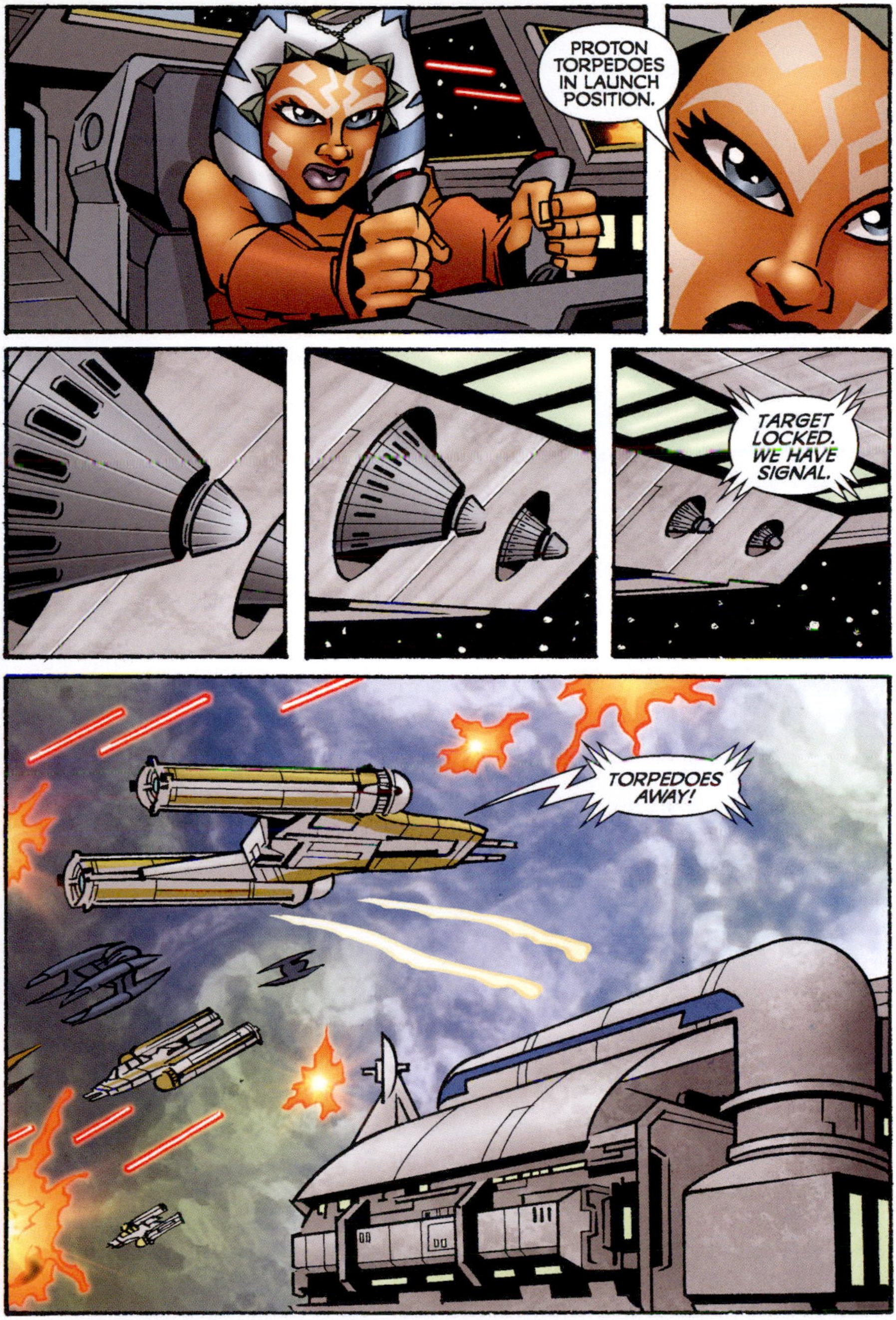
PROTON TORPEDOES IN LAUNCH POSITION.
TARGET LOCKED. WE HAVE SIGNAL.
TORPEDOES AWAY!

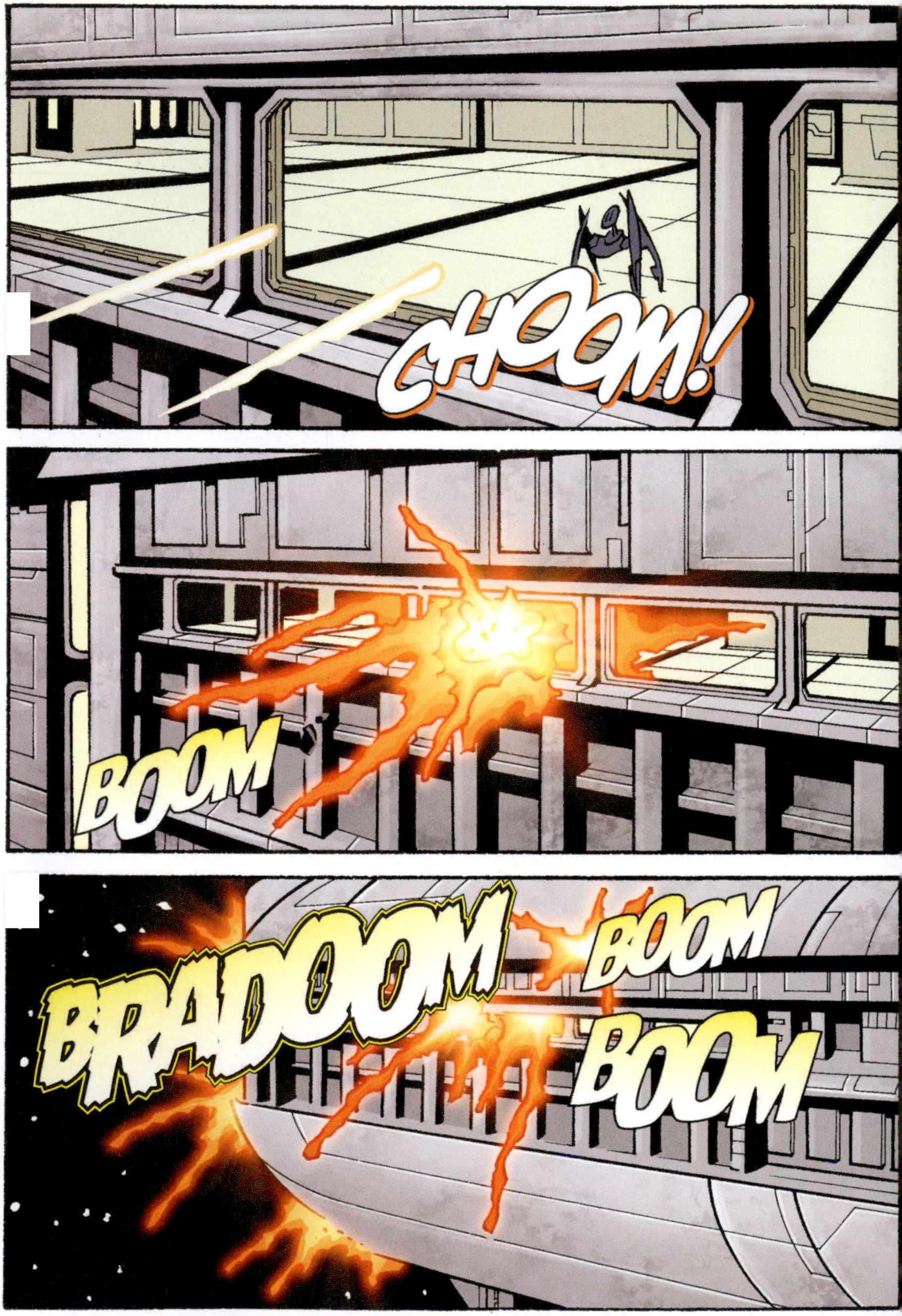
CHOOM!
BOOM
BRADOOM
BOOM
BOOM

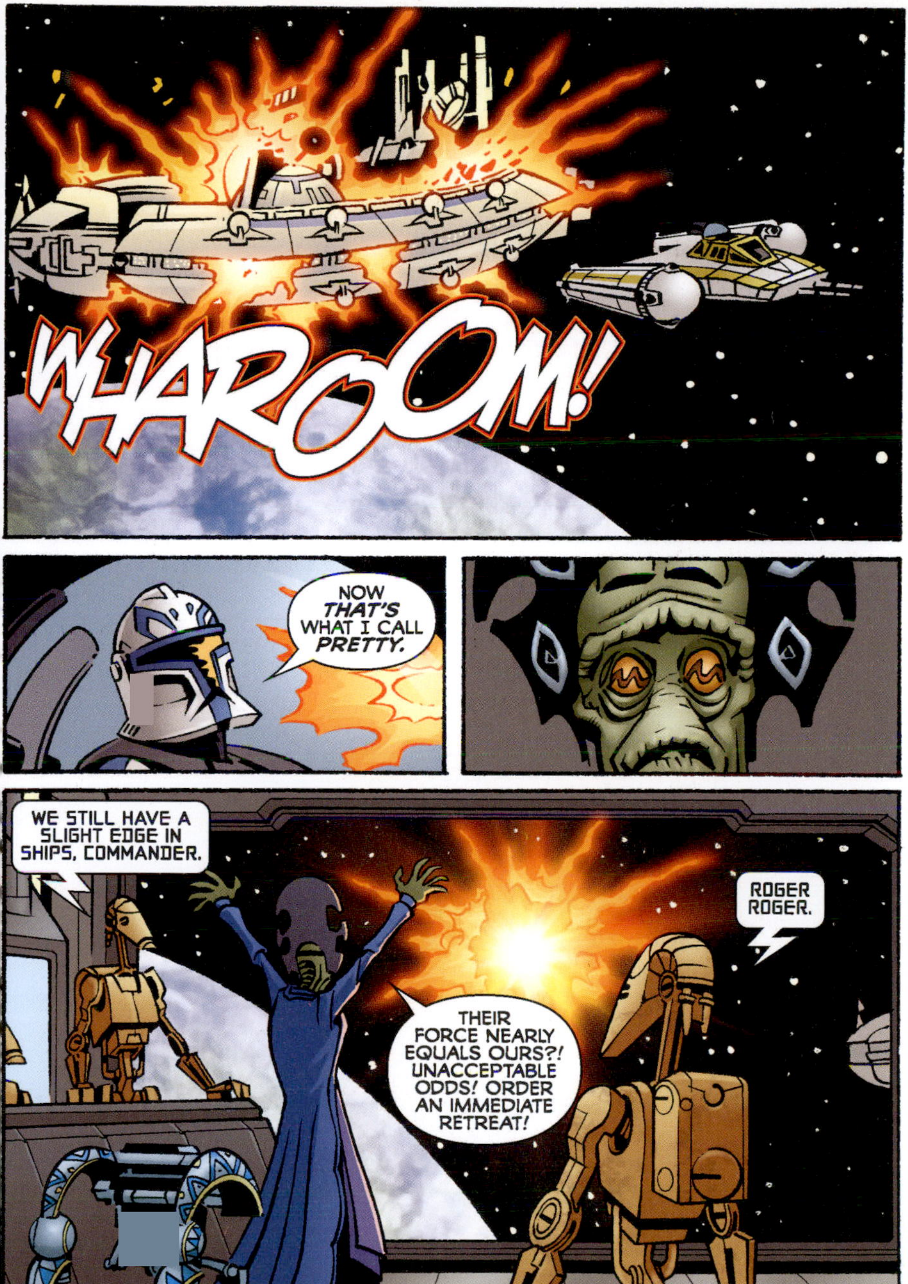
WHAROOM!
NOW THAT'S WHAT I CALL PRETTY.
WE STILL HAVE A SLIGHT EDGE IN SHIPS, COMMANDER.
THEIR FORCE NEARLY EQUALS OURS?! UNACCEPTABLE ODDS! ORDER AN IMMEDIATE RETREAT!
ROGER ROGER.

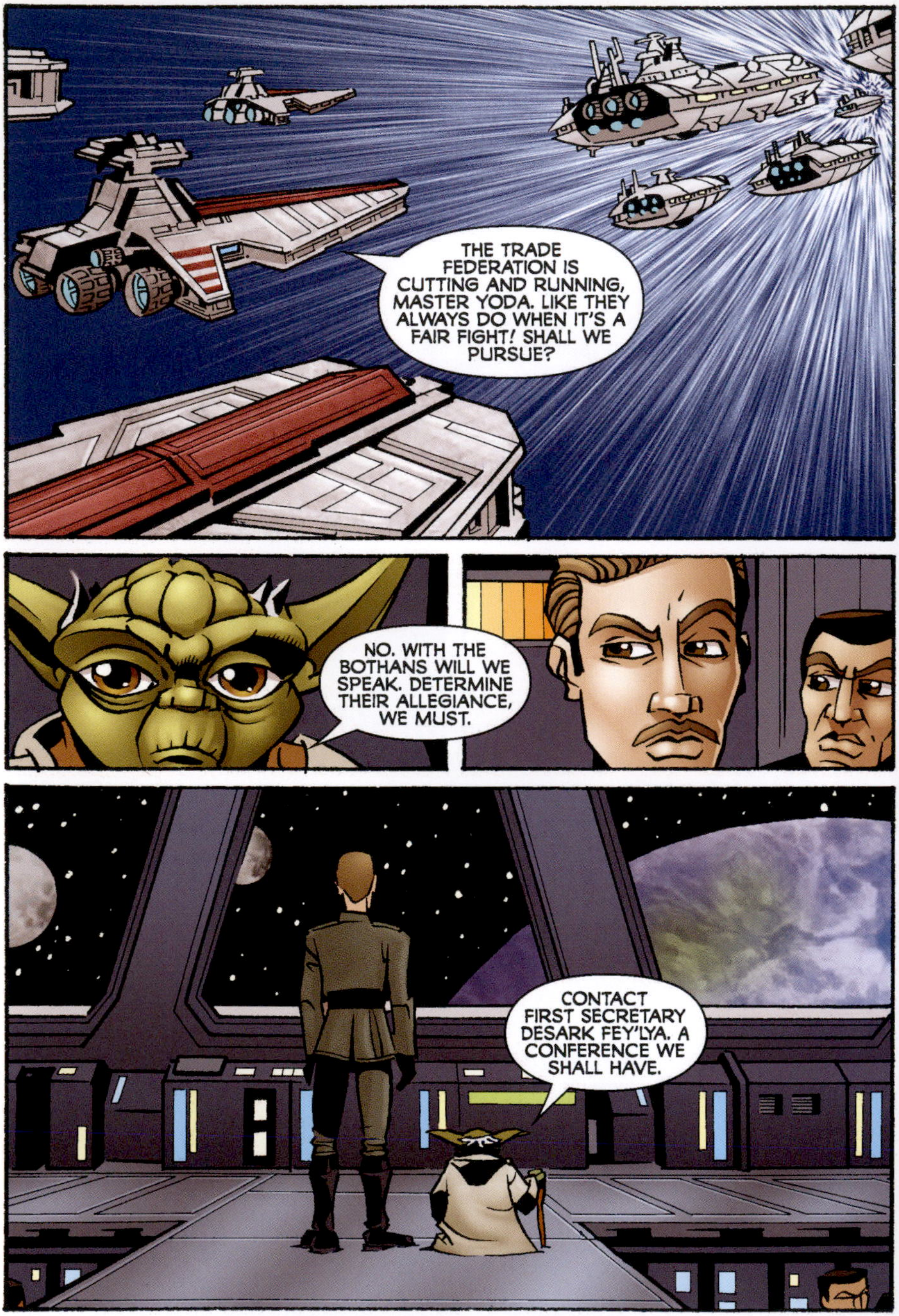
THE TRADE FEDERATION IS CUTTING AND RUNNING, MASTER YODA. LIKE THEY ALWAYS DO WHEN IT'S A FAIR FIGHT! SHALL WE PURSUE?
NO. WITH THE BOTHANS WILL WE SPEAK. DETERMINE THEIR ALLEGIANCE, WE MUST.
CONTACT FIRST SECRETARY DESARK FEY'LYA. A CONFERENCE WE SHALL HAVE.

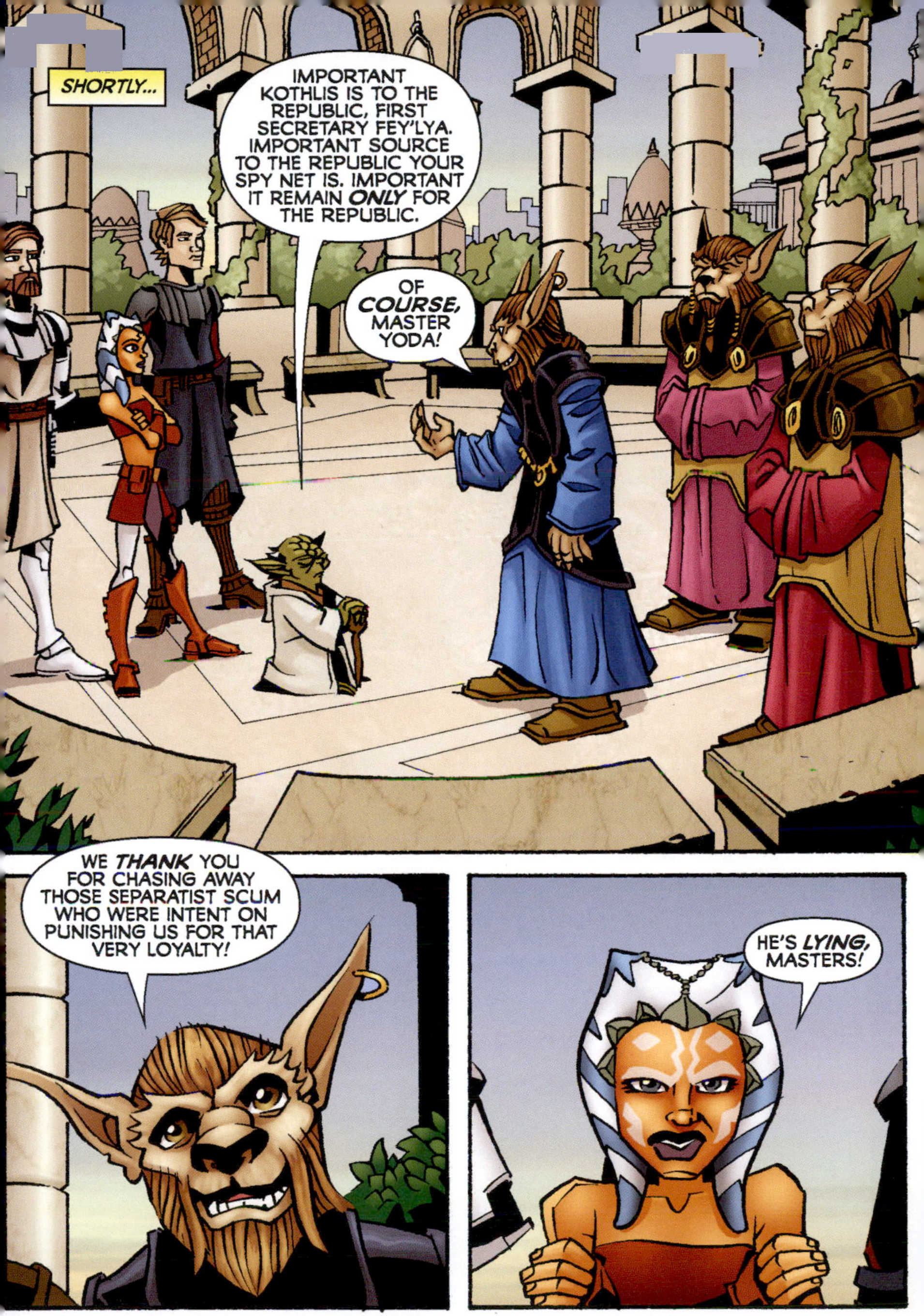
SHORTLY...
IMPORTANT KOTHLIS IS TO THE REPUBLIC, FIRST SECRETARY FEY'LYA. IMPORTANT SOURCE TO THE REPUBLIC YOUR SPY NET IS. IMPORTANT IT REMAIN ONLY FOR THE REPUBLIC.
OF COURSE, MASTER YODA!
WE THANK YOU FOR CHASING AWAY THOSE SEPARATIST SCUM WHO WERE INTENT ON PUNISHING US FOR THAT VERY LOYALTY!
HE'S LYING, MASTERS!

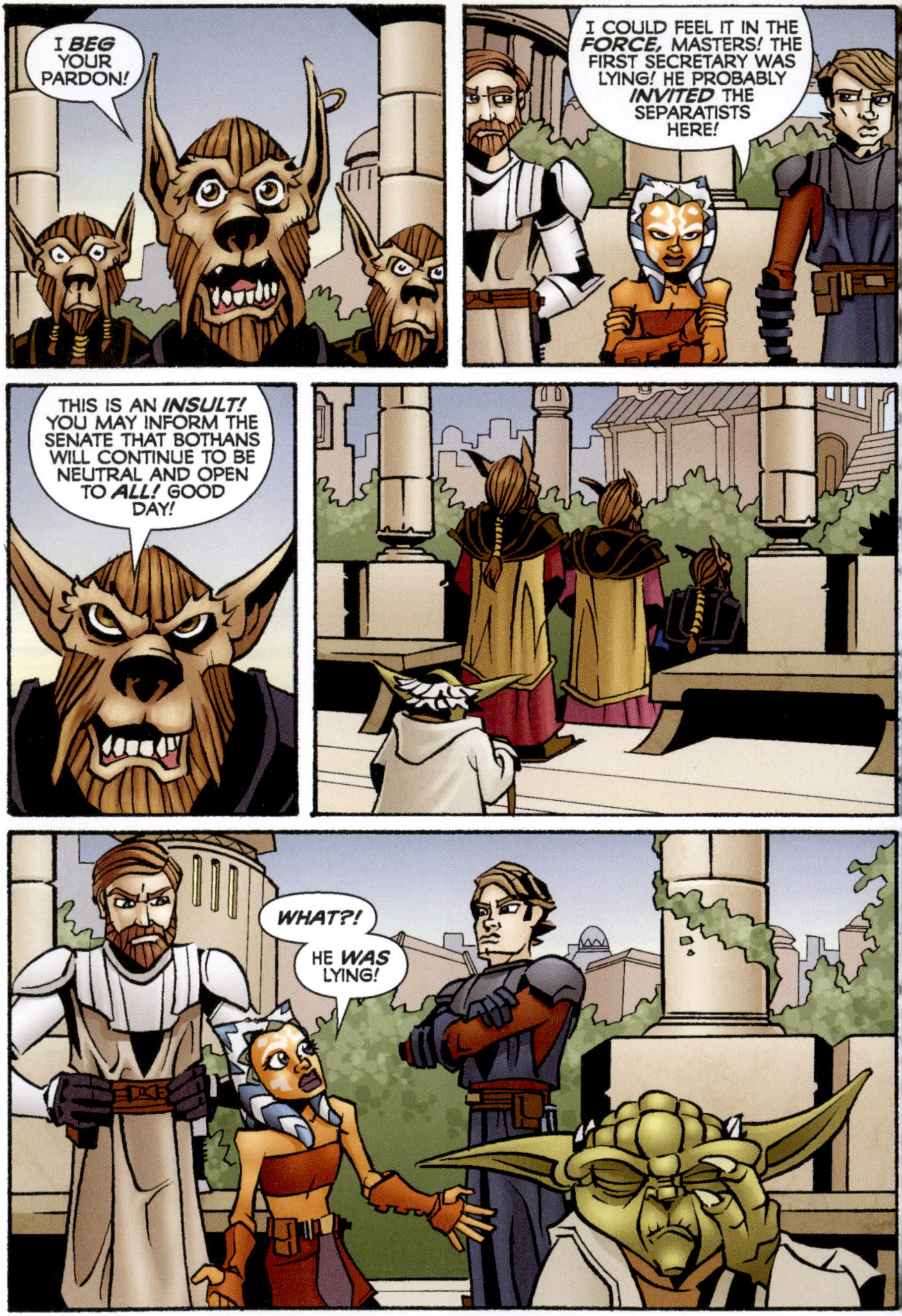
I BEG YOUR PARDON!
I COULD FEEL IT IN THE FORCE, MASTERS! THE FIRST SECRETARY WAS LYING! HE PROBABLY INVITED THE SEPARATISTS HERE!
THIS IS AN INSULT! YOU MAY INFORM THE SENATE THAT BOTHANS WILL CONTINUE TO BE NEUTRAL AND OPEN TO ALL! GOOD DAY!
WHAT?!
HE WAS LYING!

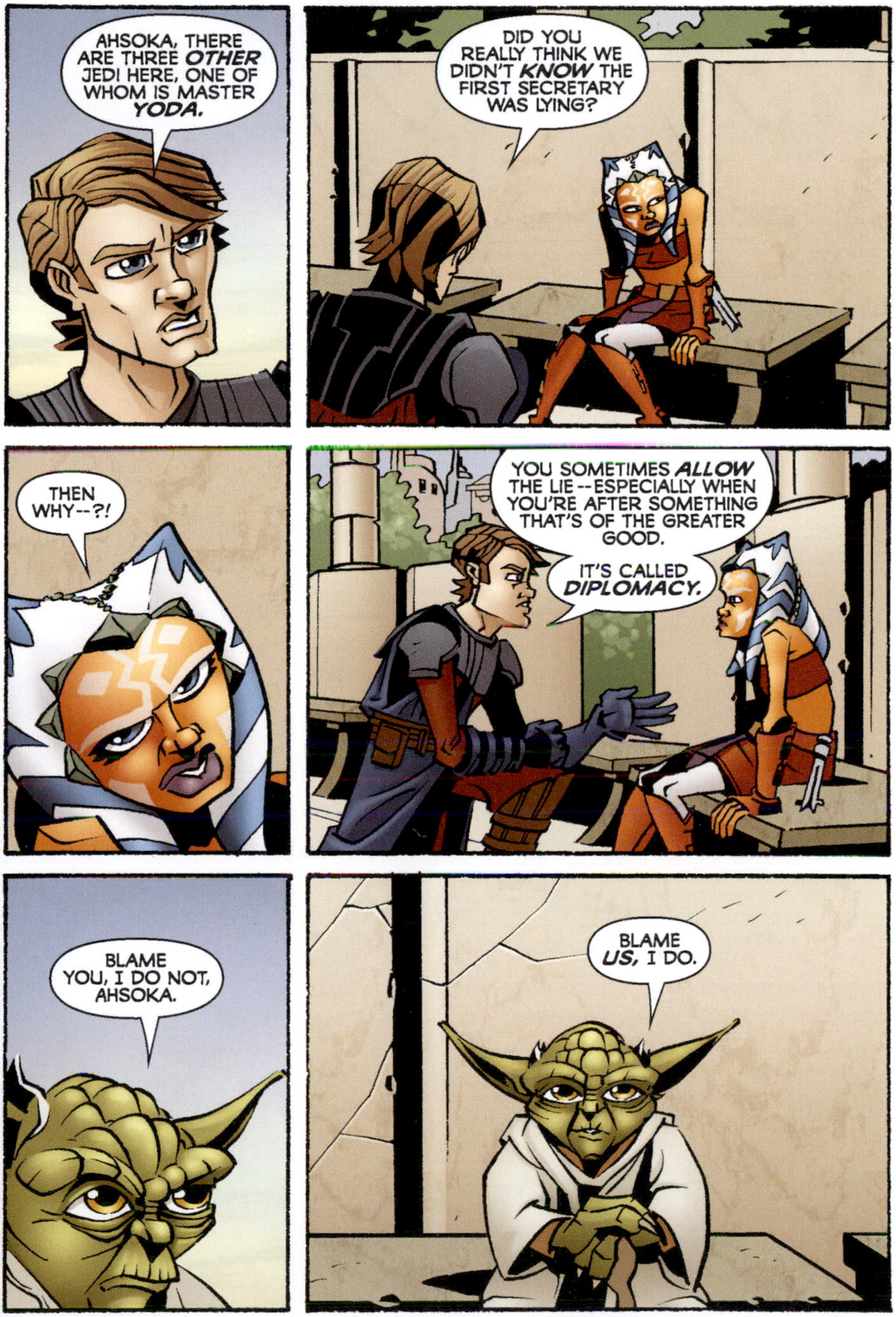
AHSOKA, THERE ARE THREE OTHER JEDI HERE, ONE OF WHOM IS MASTER YODA.
DID YOU REALLY THINK WE DIDN'T KNOW THE FIRST SECRETARY WAS LYING?
THEN WHY--?!
YOU SOMETIMES ALLOW THE LIE--ESPECIALLY WHEN YOU'RE AFTER SOMETHING THAT'S OF THE GREATER GOOD.
IT'S CALLED DIPLOMACY.
BLAME YOU, I DO NOT, AHSOKA.
BLAME US, I DO.

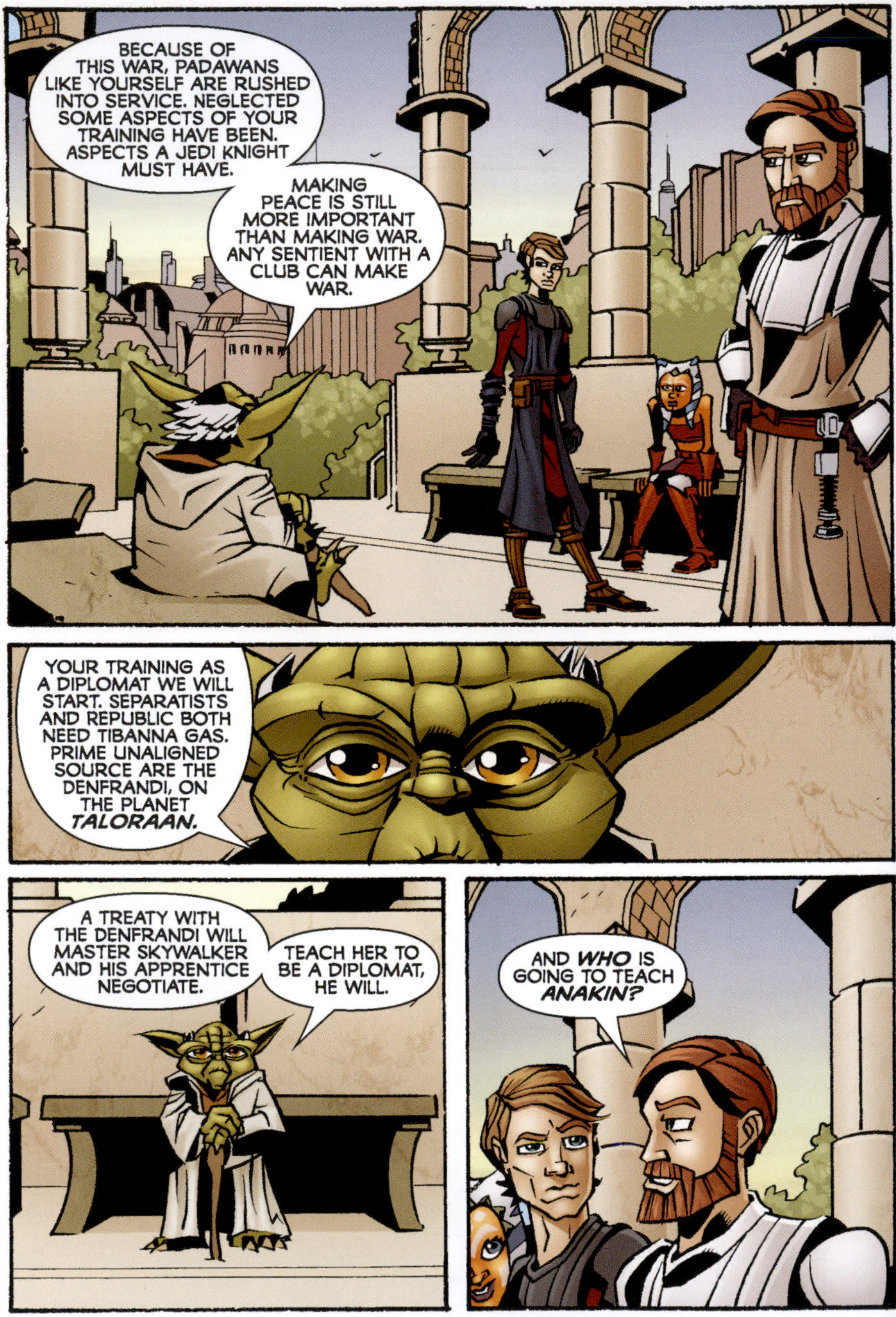
BECAUSE OF THIS WAR, PADAWANS LIKE YOURSELF ARE RUSHED INTO SERVICE. NEGLECTED SOME ASPECTS OF YOUR TRAINING HAVE BEEN. ASPECTS A JEDI KNIGHT MUST HAVE.
MAKING PEACE IS STILL MORE IMPORTANT THAN MAKING WAR. ANY SENTIENT WITH A CLUB CAN MAKE WAR.
YOUR TRAINING AS A DIPLOMAT WE WILL START. SEPARATISTS AND REPUBLIC BOTH NEED TIBANNA GAS. PRIME UNALIGNED SOURCE ARE THE DENFRANDI, ON THE PLANET ***TALORAAN.***
A TREATY WITH THE DENFRANDI WILL MASTER SKYWALKER AND HIS APPRENTICE NEGOTIATE.
TEACH HER TO BE A DIPLOMAT, HE WILL.
AND ***WHO*** IS GOING TO TEACH ***ANAKIN?***

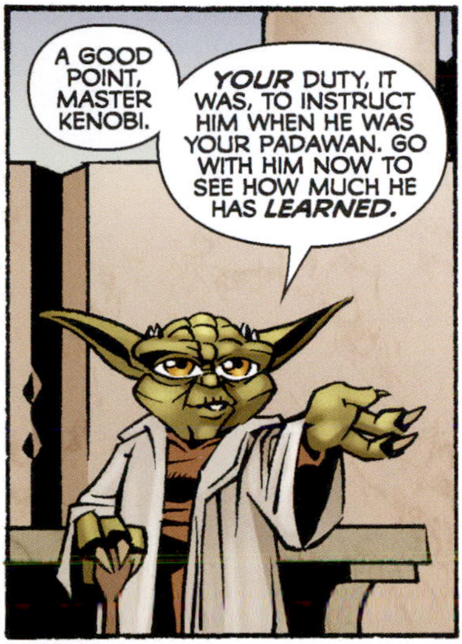
A GOOD POINT, MASTER KENOBI.
YOUR DUTY, IT WAS, TO INSTRUCT HIM WHEN HE WAS YOUR PADAWAN. GO WITH HIM NOW TO SEE HOW MUCH HE HAS LEARNED.

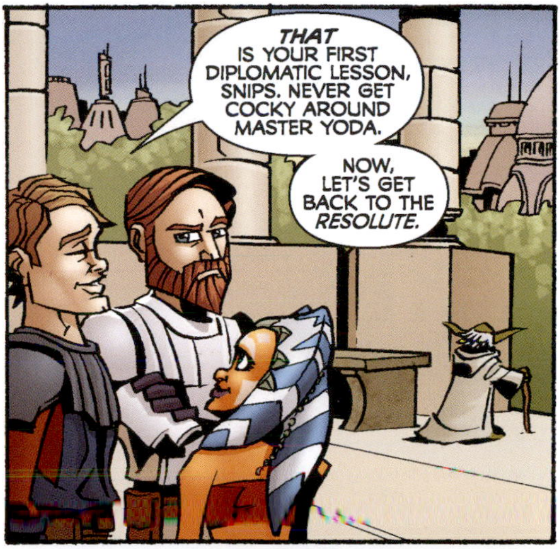
THAT IS YOUR FIRST DIPLOMATIC LESSON, SNIPS. NEVER GET COCKY AROUND MASTER YODA.
NOW, LET'S GET BACK TO THE RESOLUTE.

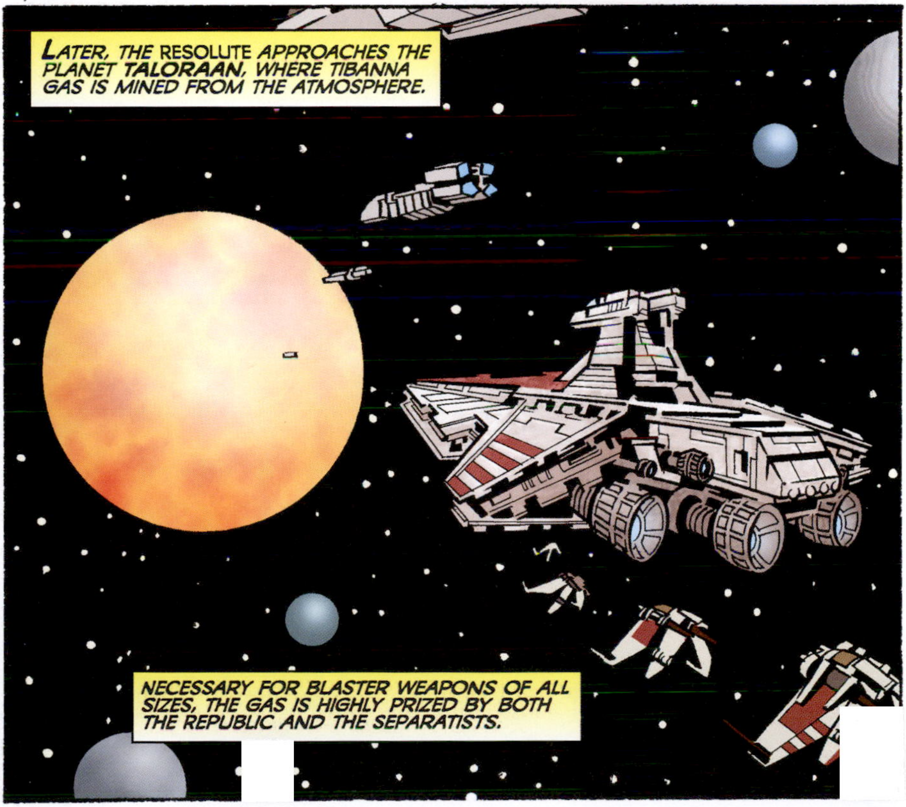
LATER, THE RESOLUTE APPROACHES THE PLANET TALORAAN, WHERE TIBANNA GAS IS MINED FROM THE ATMOSPHERE.
NECESSARY FOR BLASTER WEAPONS OF ALL SIZES, THE GAS IS HIGHLY PRIZED BY BOTH THE REPUBLIC AND THE SEPARATISTS.

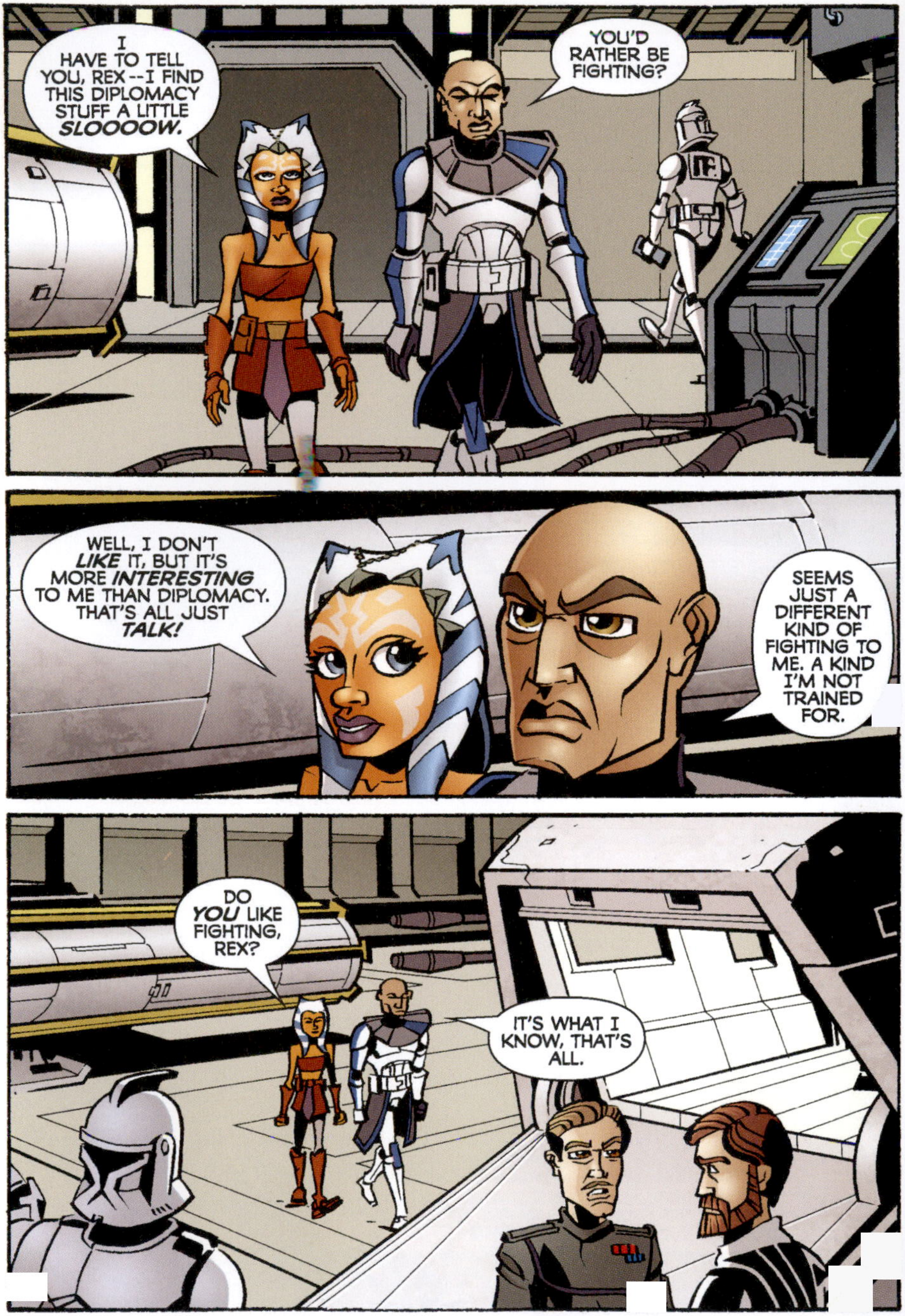
I HAVE TO TELL YOU, REX--I FIND THIS DIPLOMACY STUFF A LITTLE SLOOOOW.
YOU'D RATHER BE FIGHTING?
WELL, I DON'T LIKE IT, BUT IT'S MORE INTERESTING TO ME THAN DIPLOMACY. THAT'S ALL JUST TALK!
SEEMS JUST A DIFFERENT KIND OF FIGHTING TO ME. A KIND I'M NOT TRAINED FOR.
DO YOU LIKE FIGHTING, REX?
IT'S WHAT I KNOW, THAT'S ALL.

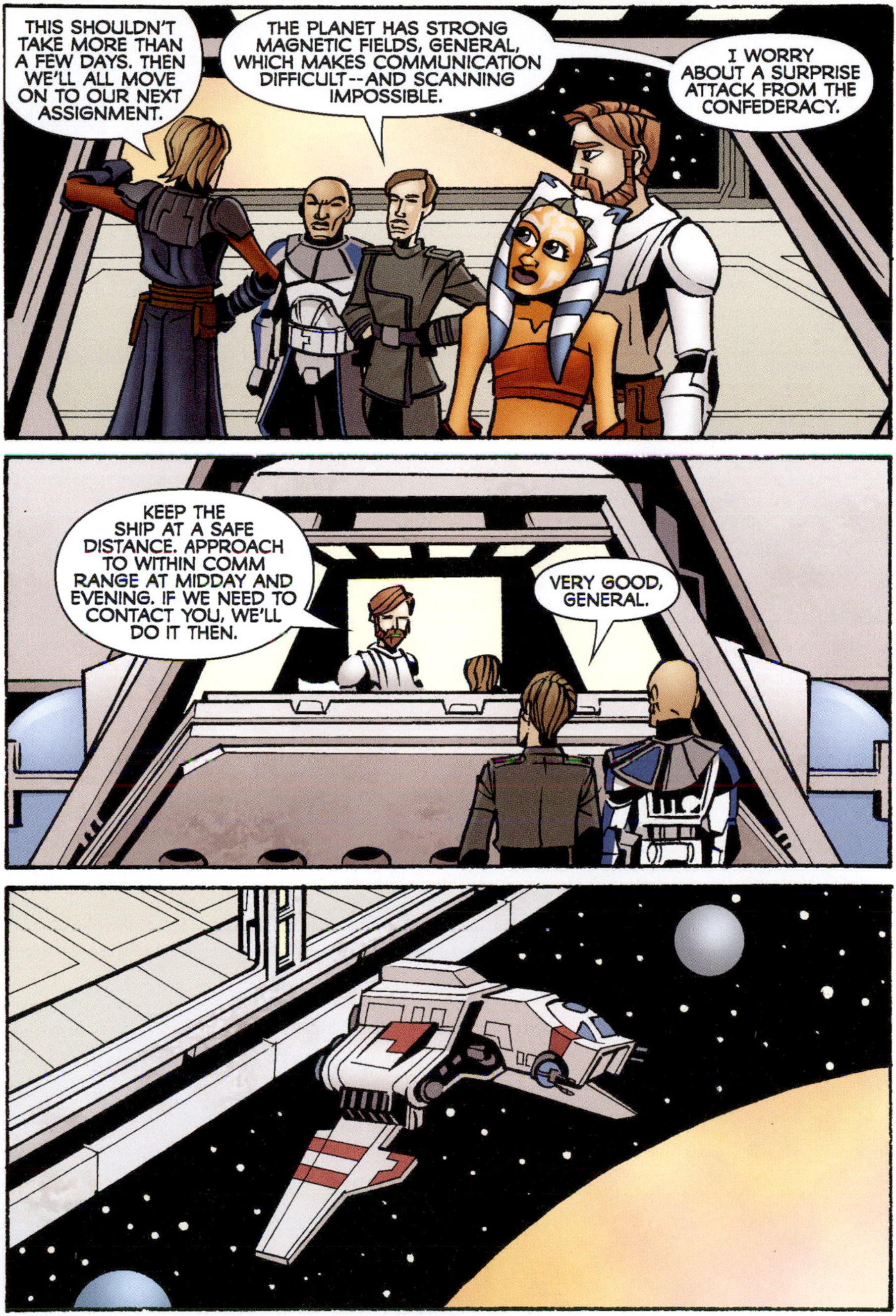
THIS SHOULDN'T TAKE MORE THAN A FEW DAYS. THEN WE'LL ALL MOVE ON TO OUR NEXT ASSIGNMENT.
THE PLANET HAS STRONG MAGNETIC FIELDS, GENERAL, WHICH MAKES COMMUNICATION DIFFICULT--AND SCANNING IMPOSSIBLE.
I WORRY ABOUT A SURPRISE ATTACK FROM THE CONFEDERACY.
KEEP THE SHIP AT A SAFE DISTANCE. APPROACH TO WITHIN COMM RANGE AT MIDDAY AND EVENING. IF WE NEED TO CONTACT YOU, WE'LL DO IT THEN.
VERY GOOD, GENERAL.

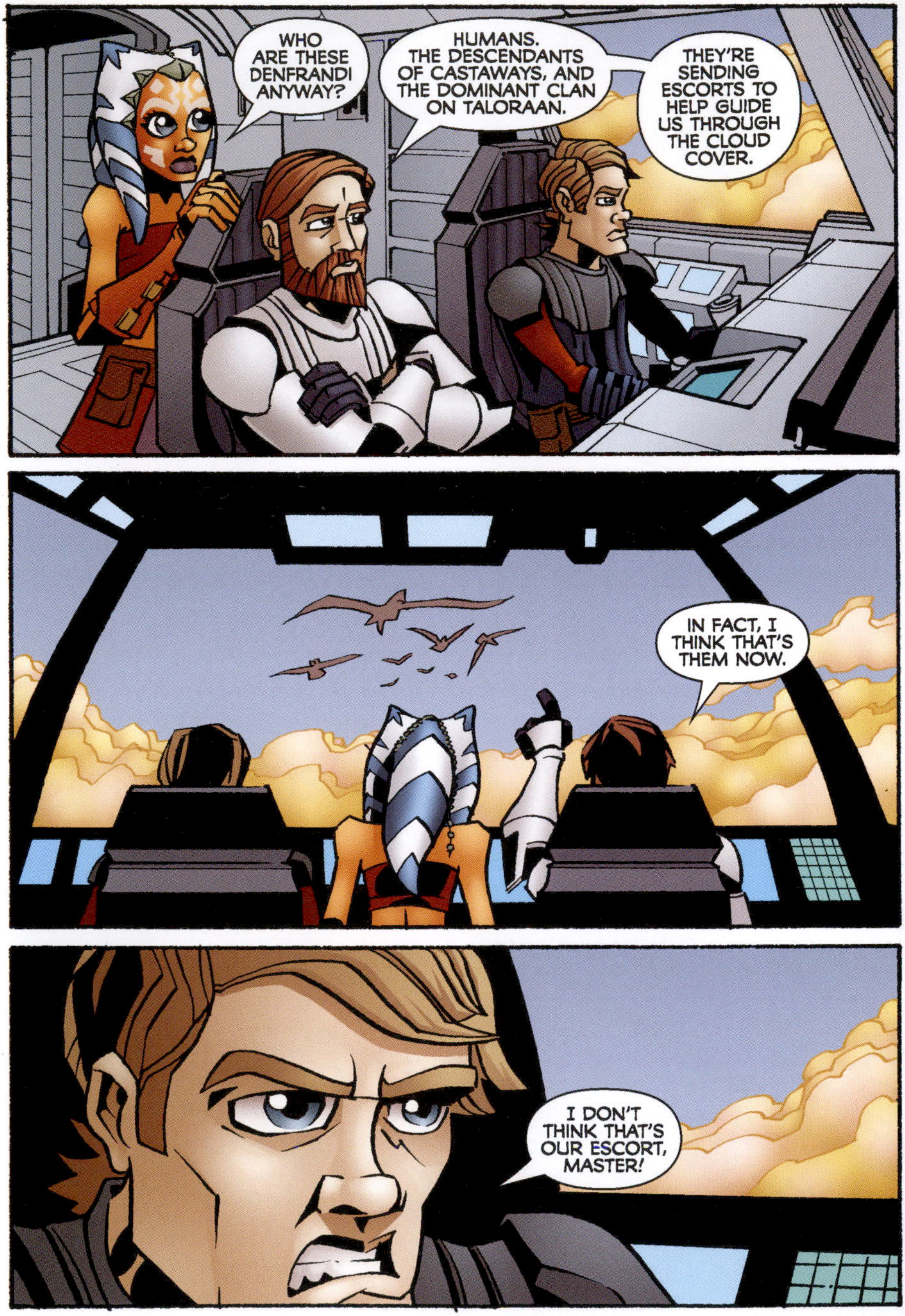
WHO ARE THESE DENFRANDI ANYWAY?
HUMANS. THE DESCENDANTS OF CASTAWAYS, AND THE DOMINANT CLAN ON TALORAAN.
THEY'RE SENDING ESCORTS TO HELP GUIDE US THROUGH THE CLOUD COVER.
IN FACT, I THINK THAT'S THEM NOW.
I DON'T THINK THAT'S OUR ESCORT, MASTER!

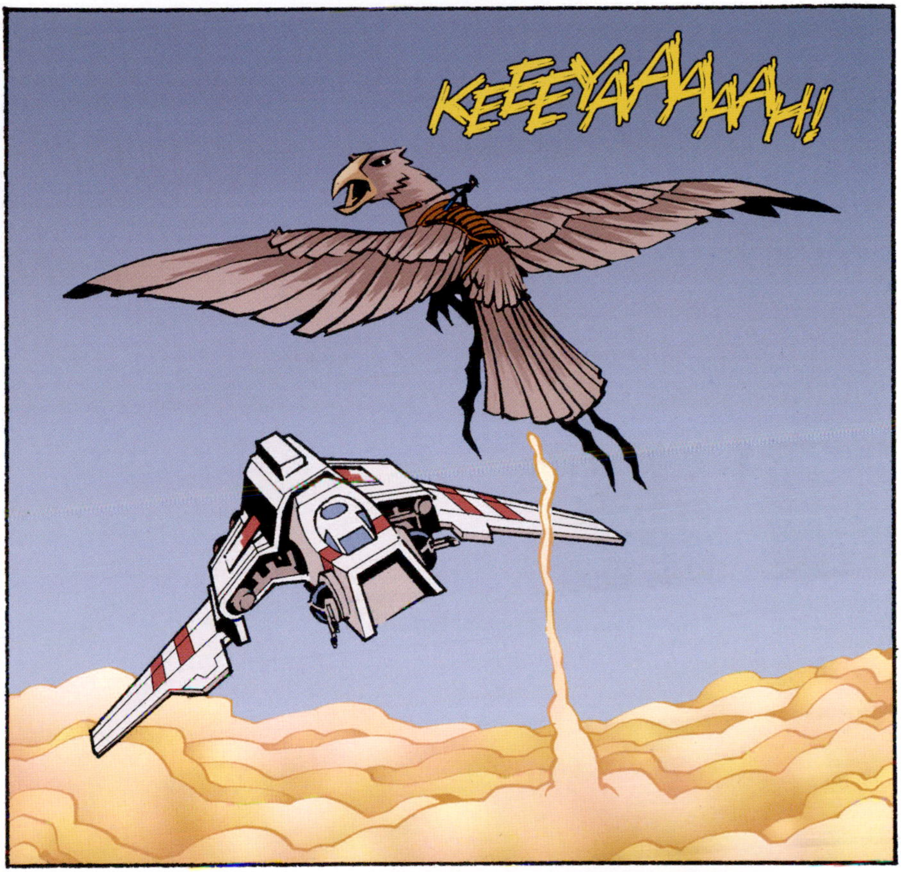
KEEEYAAAAAH!

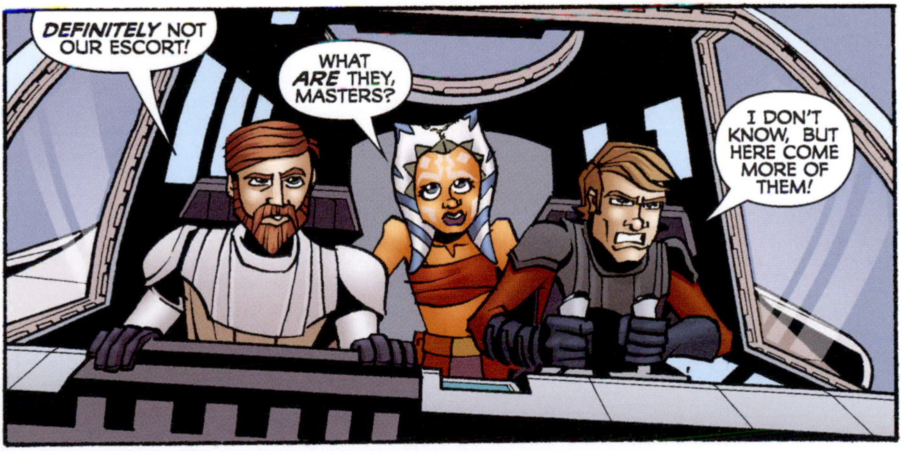
DEFINITELY NOT OUR ESCORT!
WHAT ARE THEY, MASTERS?
I DON'T KNOW, BUT HERE COME MORE OF THEM!

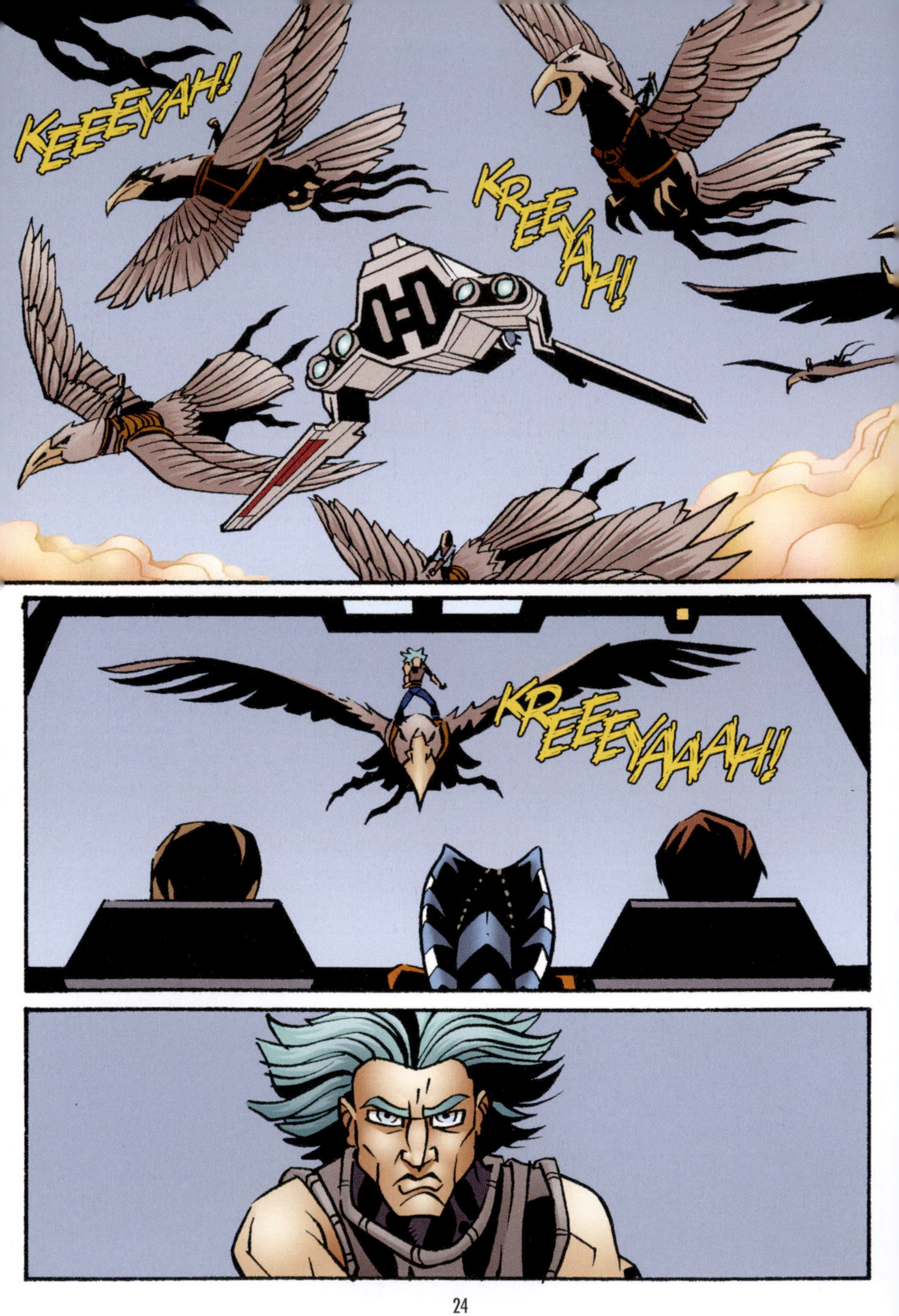
KEEEEYAH!
KREEEYAH!
KREEEYAAAH!

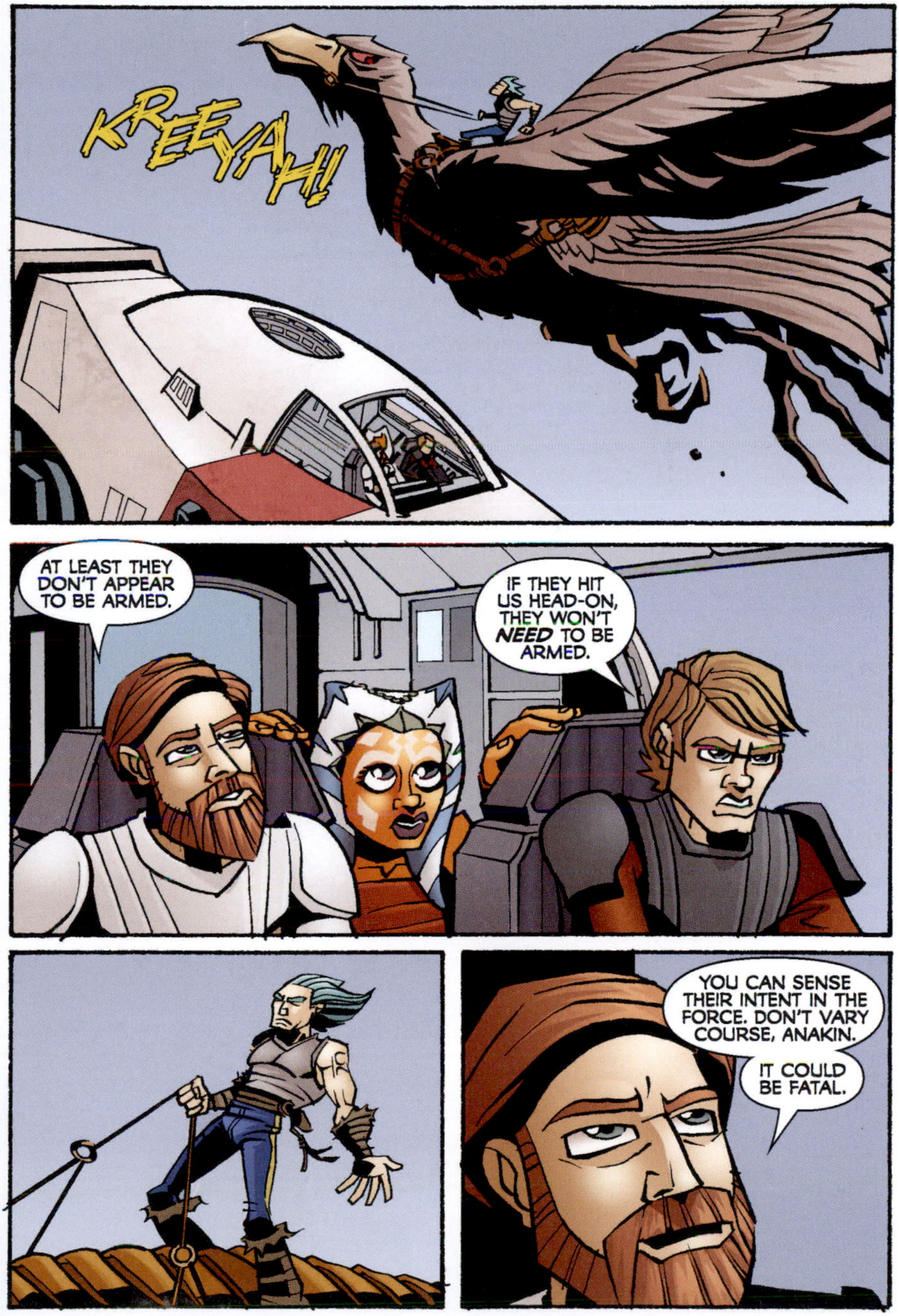
KREEYAH!
AT LEAST THEY DON'T APPEAR TO BE ARMED.
IF THEY HIT US HEAD-ON, THEY WON'T *NEED* TO BE ARMED.
YOU CAN SENSE THEIR INTENT IN THE FORCE. DON'T VARY COURSE, ANAKIN.
IT COULD BE FATAL.

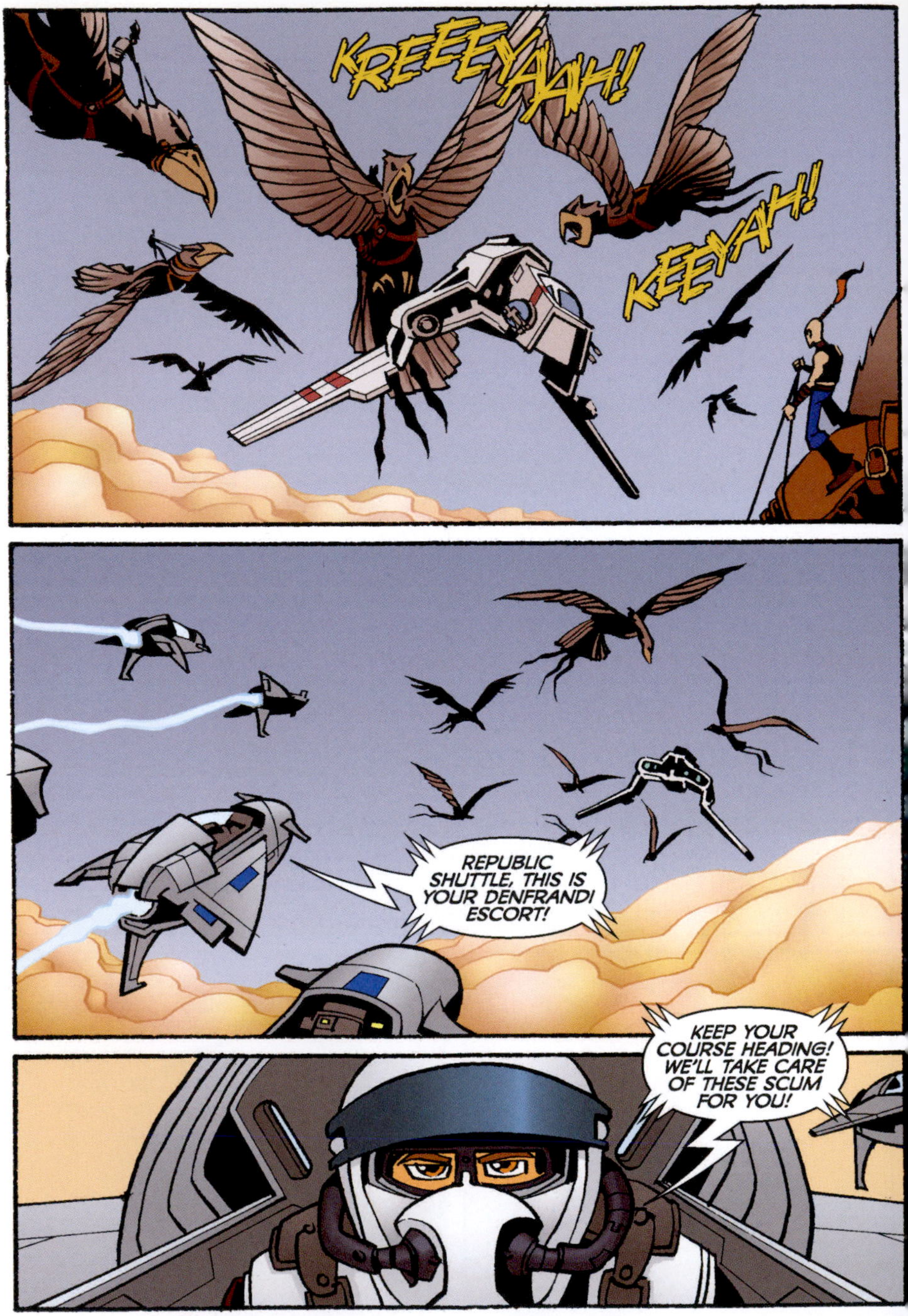
KREEEEYAAH!
KEEYAH!
REPUBLIC SHUTTLE, THIS IS YOUR DENFRANDI ESCORT!
KEEP YOUR COURSE HEADING! WE'LL TAKE CARE OF THESE SCUM FOR YOU!

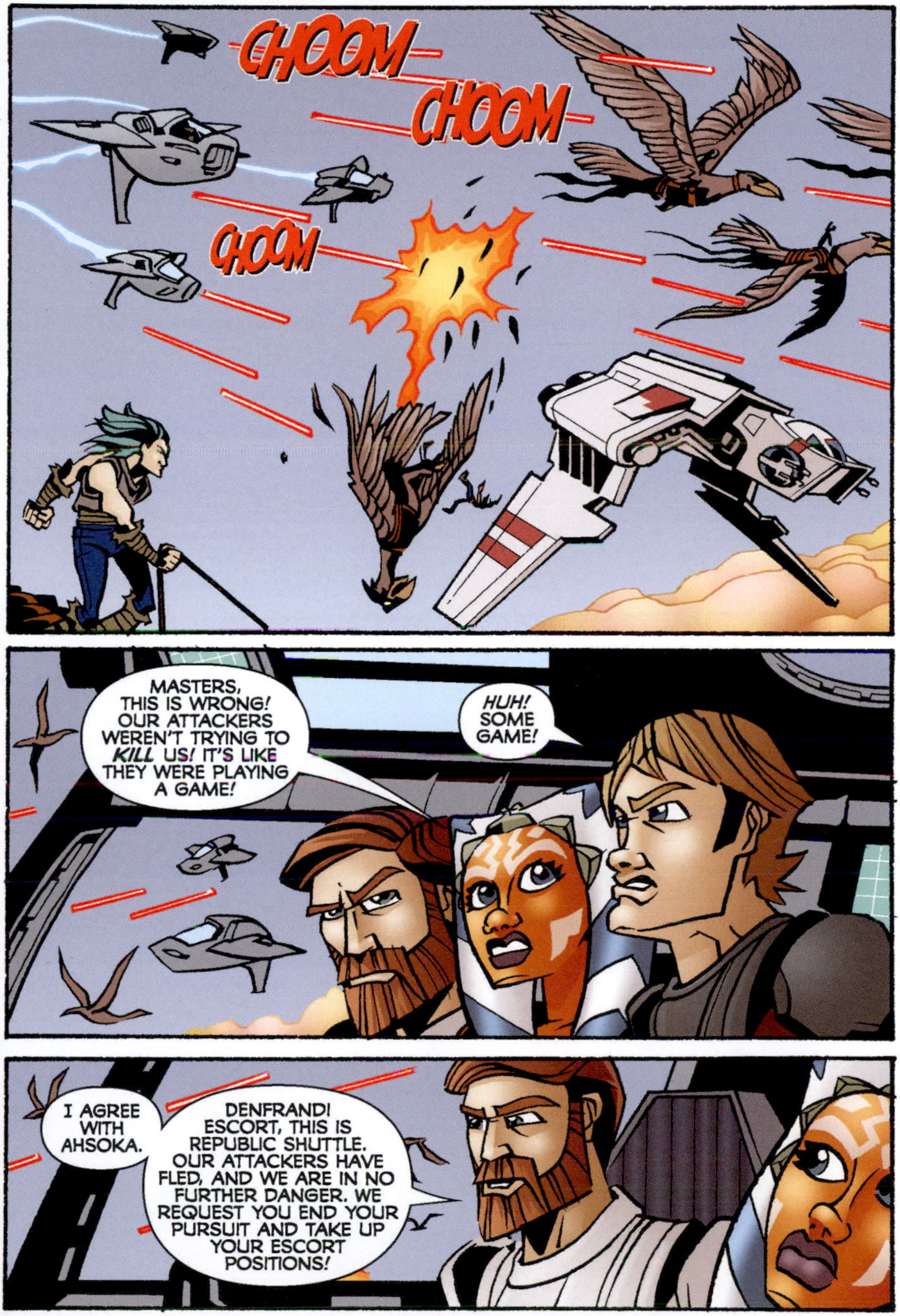
CHOOM
CHOOM
CHOOM
MASTERS, THIS IS WRONG! OUR ATTACKERS WEREN'T TRYING TO *KILL* US! IT'S LIKE THEY WERE PLAYING A GAME!
HUH! SOME GAME!
I AGREE WITH AHSOKA.
DENFRAND! ESCORT, THIS IS REPUBLIC SHUTTLE. OUR ATTACKERS HAVE FLED, AND WE ARE IN NO FURTHER DANGER. WE REQUEST YOU END YOUR PURSUIT AND TAKE UP YOUR ESCORT POSITIONS!

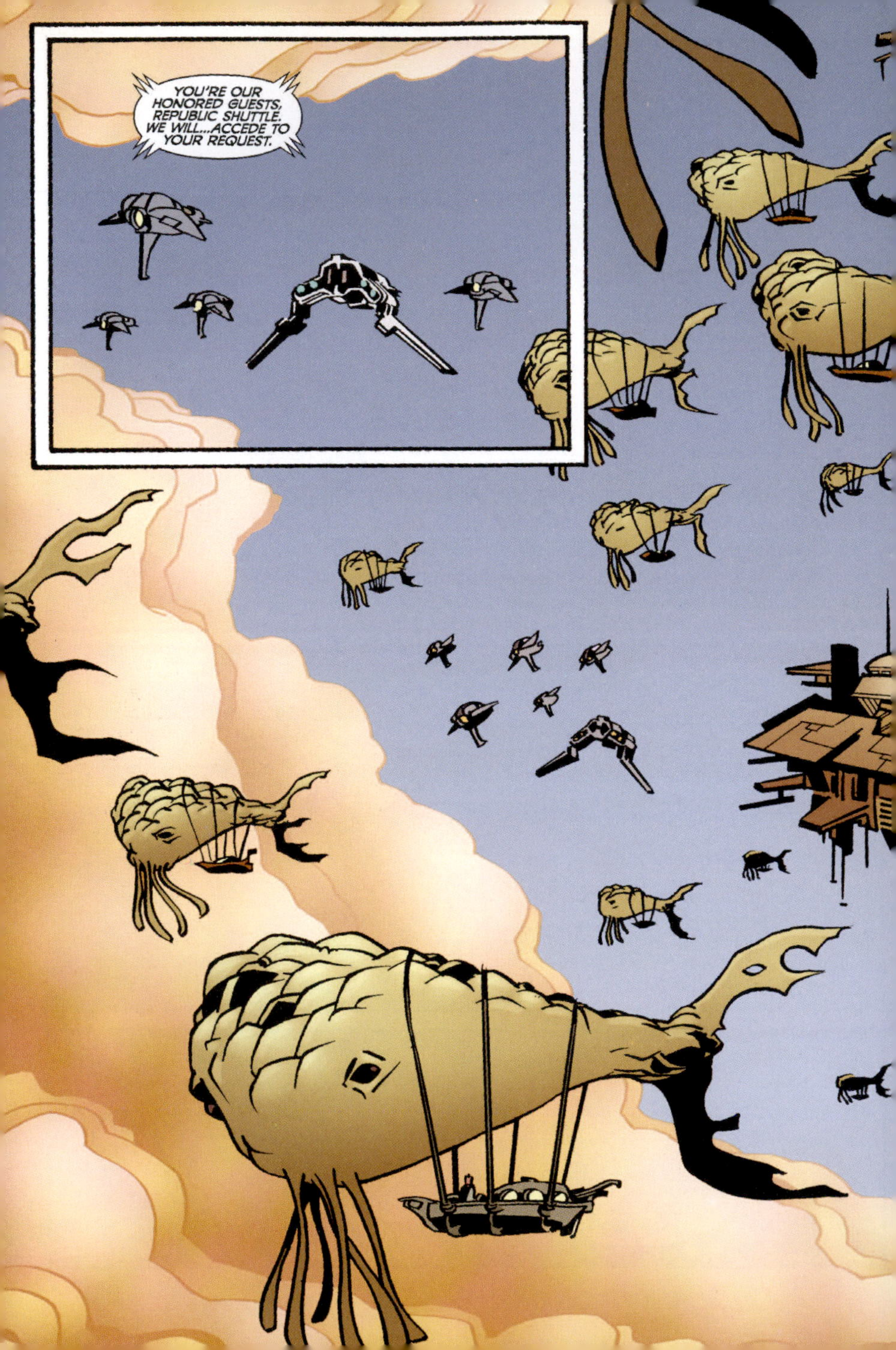
YOU'RE OUR HONORED GUESTS, REPUBLIC SHUTTLE. WE WILL...ACCEDE TO YOUR REQUEST.

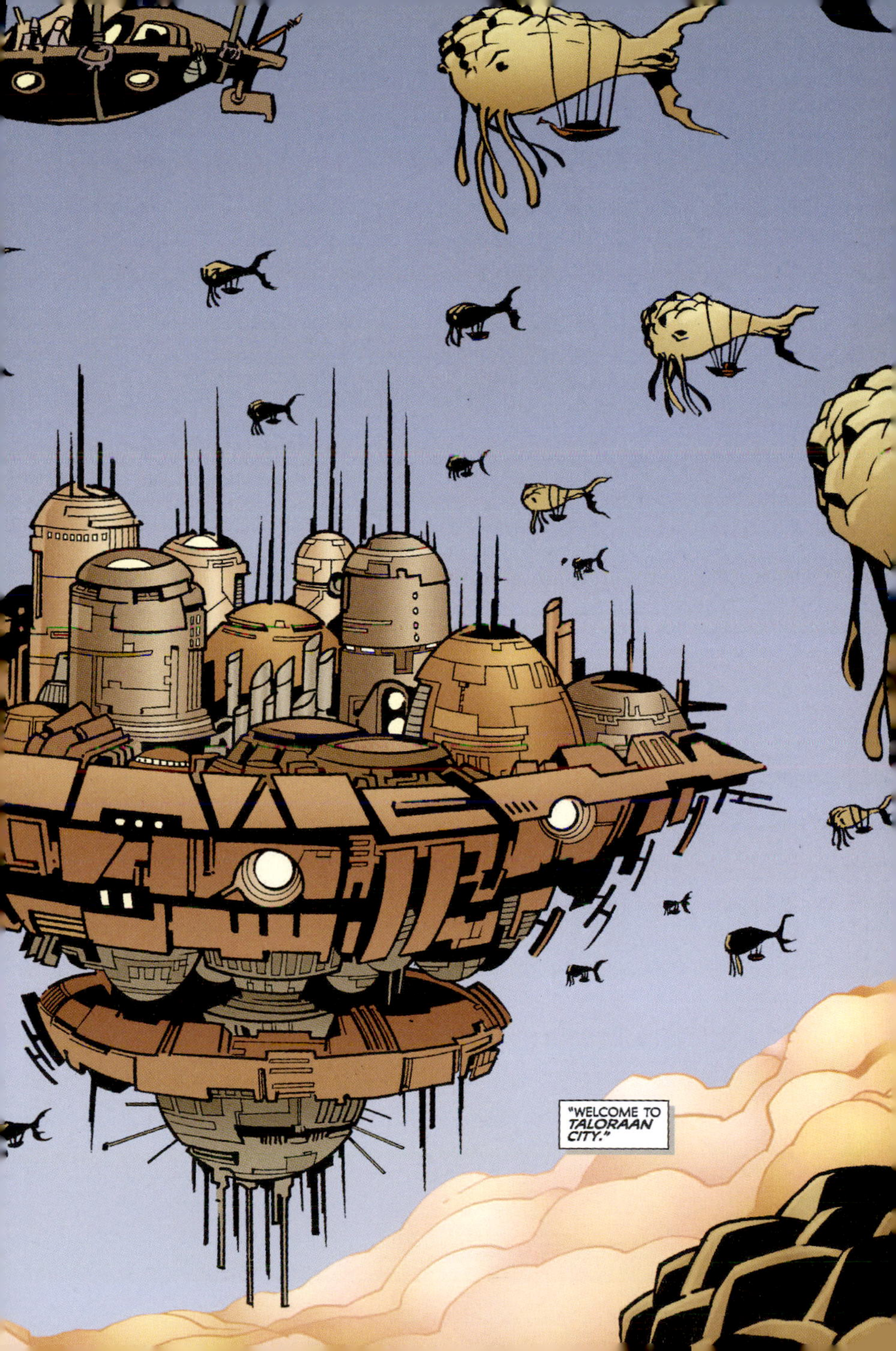
"WELCOME TO TALORAAN CITY."

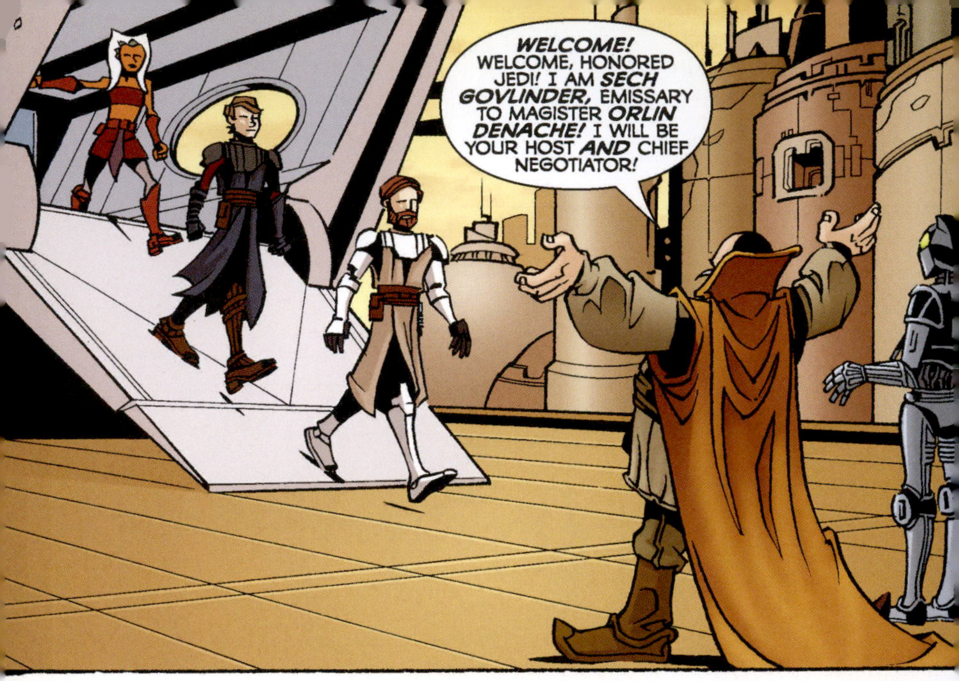
WELCOME! WELCOME, HONORED JEDI! I AM SECH GOVLINDER, EMISSARY TO MAGISTER ORLIN DENACHE! I WILL BE YOUR HOST AND CHIEF NEGOTIATOR!

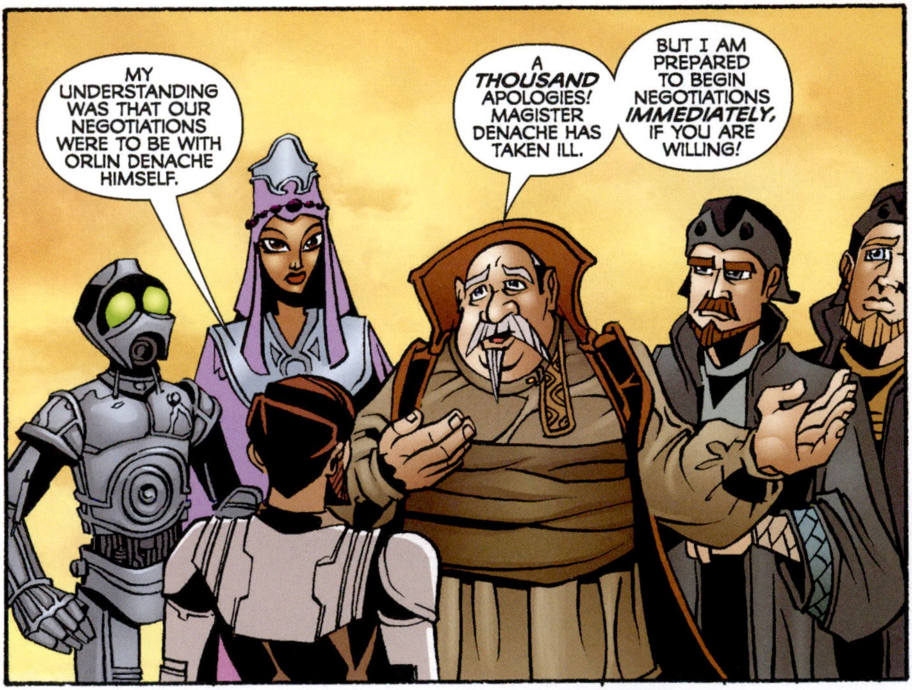
MY UNDERSTANDING WAS THAT OUR NEGOTIATIONS WERE TO BE WITH ORLIN DENACHE HIMSELF.
A THOUSAND APOLOGIES! MAGISTER DENACHE HAS TAKEN ILL.
BUT I AM PREPARED TO BEGIN NEGOTIATIONS IMMEDIATELY, IF YOU ARE WILLING!

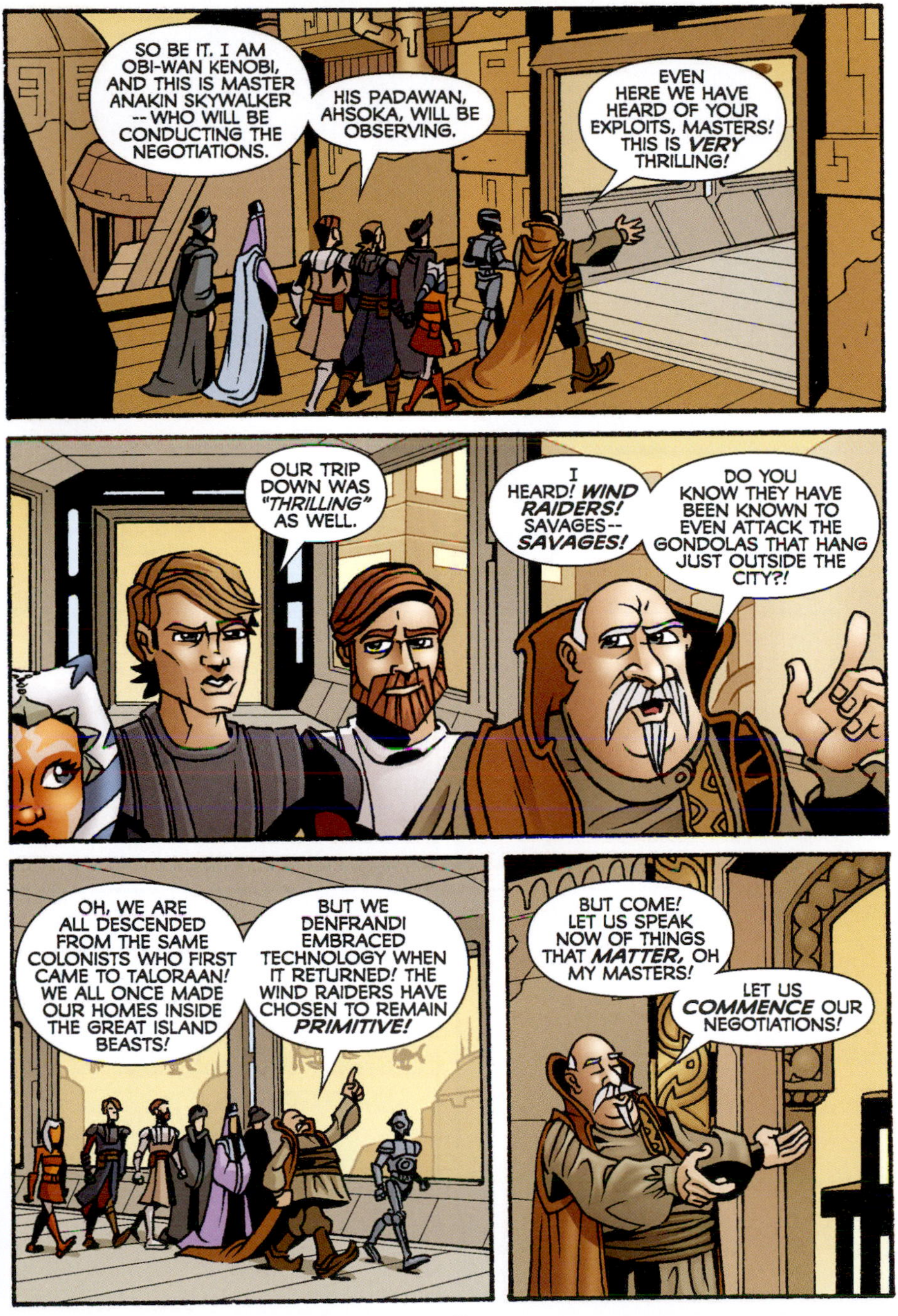
SO BE IT. I AM OBI-WAN KENOBI, AND THIS IS MASTER ANAKIN SKYWALKER -- WHO WILL BE CONDUCTING THE NEGOTIATIONS.
HIS PADAWAN, AHSOKA, WILL BE OBSERVING.
EVEN HERE WE HAVE HEARD OF YOUR EXPLOITS, MASTERS! THIS IS *VERY* THRILLING!
OUR TRIP DOWN WAS *"THRILLING"* AS WELL.
I HEARD! *WIND RAIDERS!* SAVAGES-- *SAVAGES!*
DO YOU KNOW THEY HAVE BEEN KNOWN TO EVEN ATTACK THE GONDOLAS THAT HANG JUST OUTSIDE THE CITY?!
OH, WE ARE ALL DESCENDED FROM THE SAME COLONISTS WHO FIRST CAME TO TALORAAN! WE ALL ONCE MADE OUR HOMES INSIDE THE GREAT ISLAND BEASTS!
BUT WE DENFRANDI EMBRACED TECHNOLOGY WHEN IT RETURNED! THE WIND RAIDERS HAVE CHOSEN TO REMAIN *PRIMITIVE!*
BUT COME! LET US SPEAK NOW OF THINGS THAT *MATTER,* OH MY MASTERS!
LET US *COMMENCE* OUR NEGOTIATIONS!

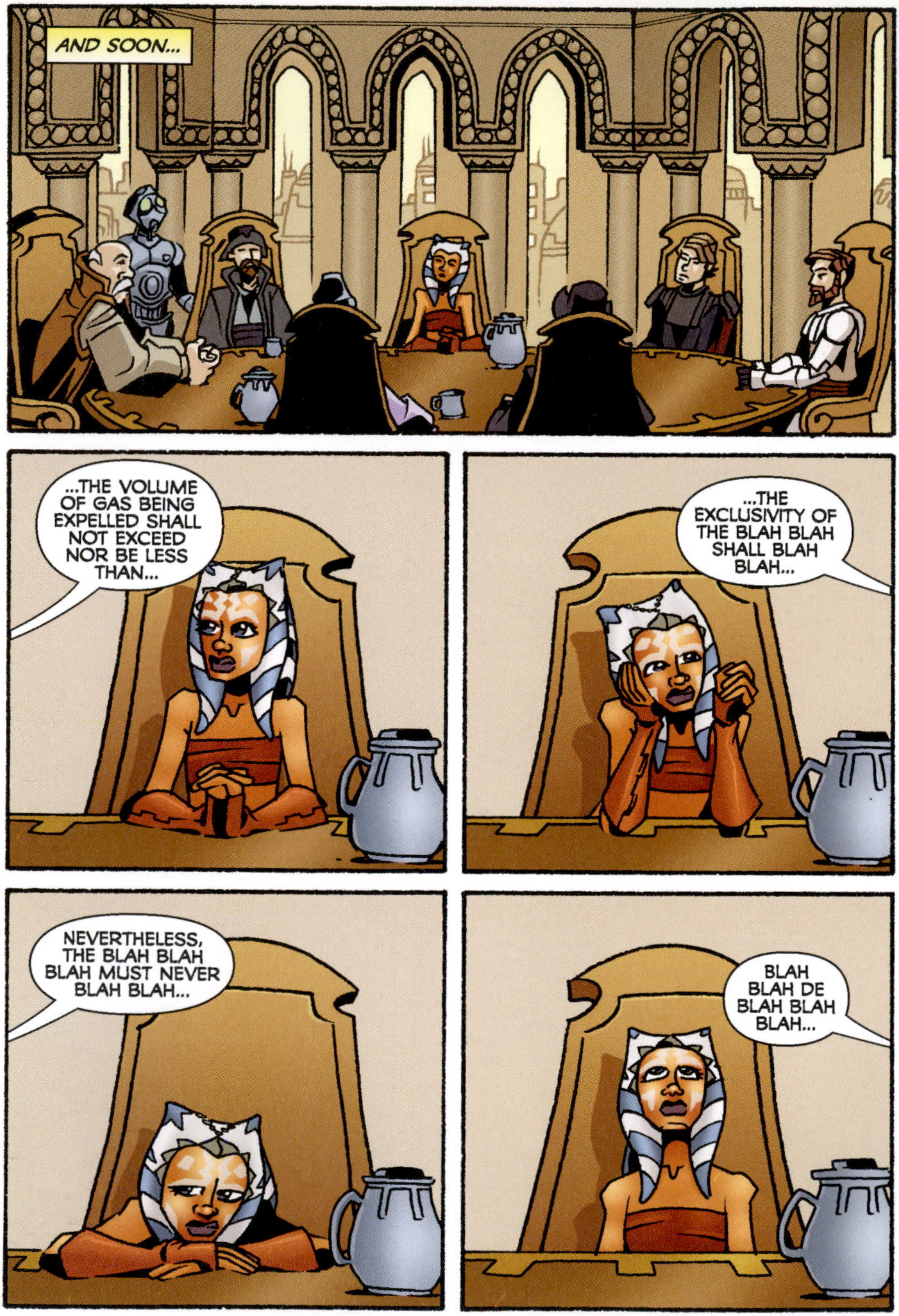
AND SOON...
...THE VOLUME OF GAS BEING EXPELLED SHALL NOT EXCEED NOR BE LESS THAN...
...THE EXCLUSIVITY OF THE BLAH BLAH SHALL BLAH BLAH...
NEVERTHELESS, THE BLAH BLAH BLAH MUST NEVER BLAH BLAH...
BLAH BLAH DE BLAH BLAH BLAH...

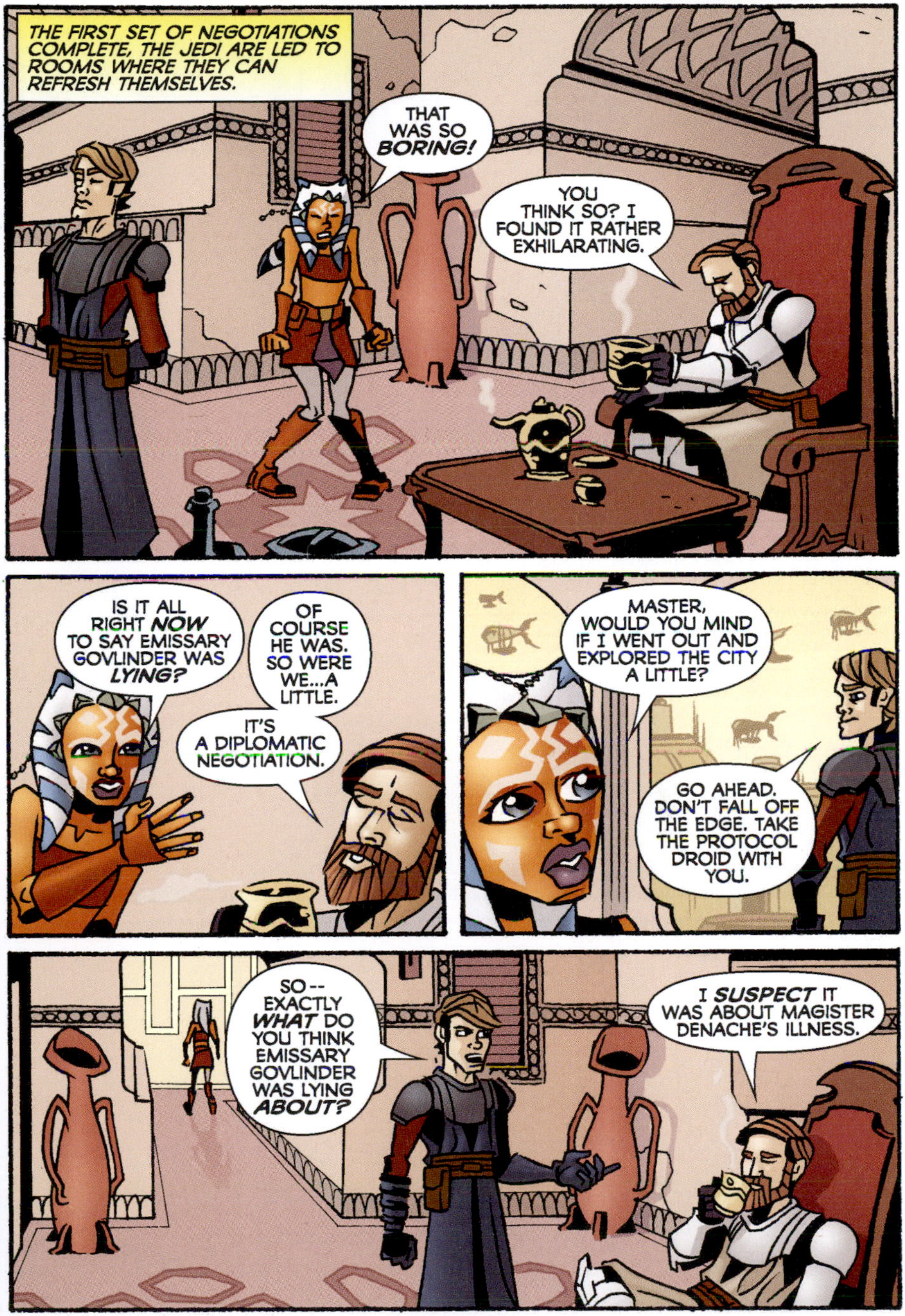
THE FIRST SET OF NEGOTIATIONS COMPLETE, THE JEDI ARE LED TO ROOMS WHERE THEY CAN REFRESH THEMSELVES.
THAT WAS SO BORING!
YOU THINK SO? I FOUND IT RATHER EXHILARATING.
IS IT ALL RIGHT NOW TO SAY EMISSARY GOVLINDER WAS LYING?
OF COURSE HE WAS. SO WERE WE...A LITTLE.
IT'S A DIPLOMATIC NEGOTIATION.
MASTER, WOULD YOU MIND IF I WENT OUT AND EXPLORED THE CITY A LITTLE?
GO AHEAD. DON'T FALL OFF THE EDGE. TAKE THE PROTOCOL DROID WITH YOU.
SO-- EXACTLY WHAT DO YOU THINK EMISSARY GOVLINDER WAS LYING ABOUT?
I SUSPECT IT WAS ABOUT MAGISTER DENACHE'S ILLNESS.

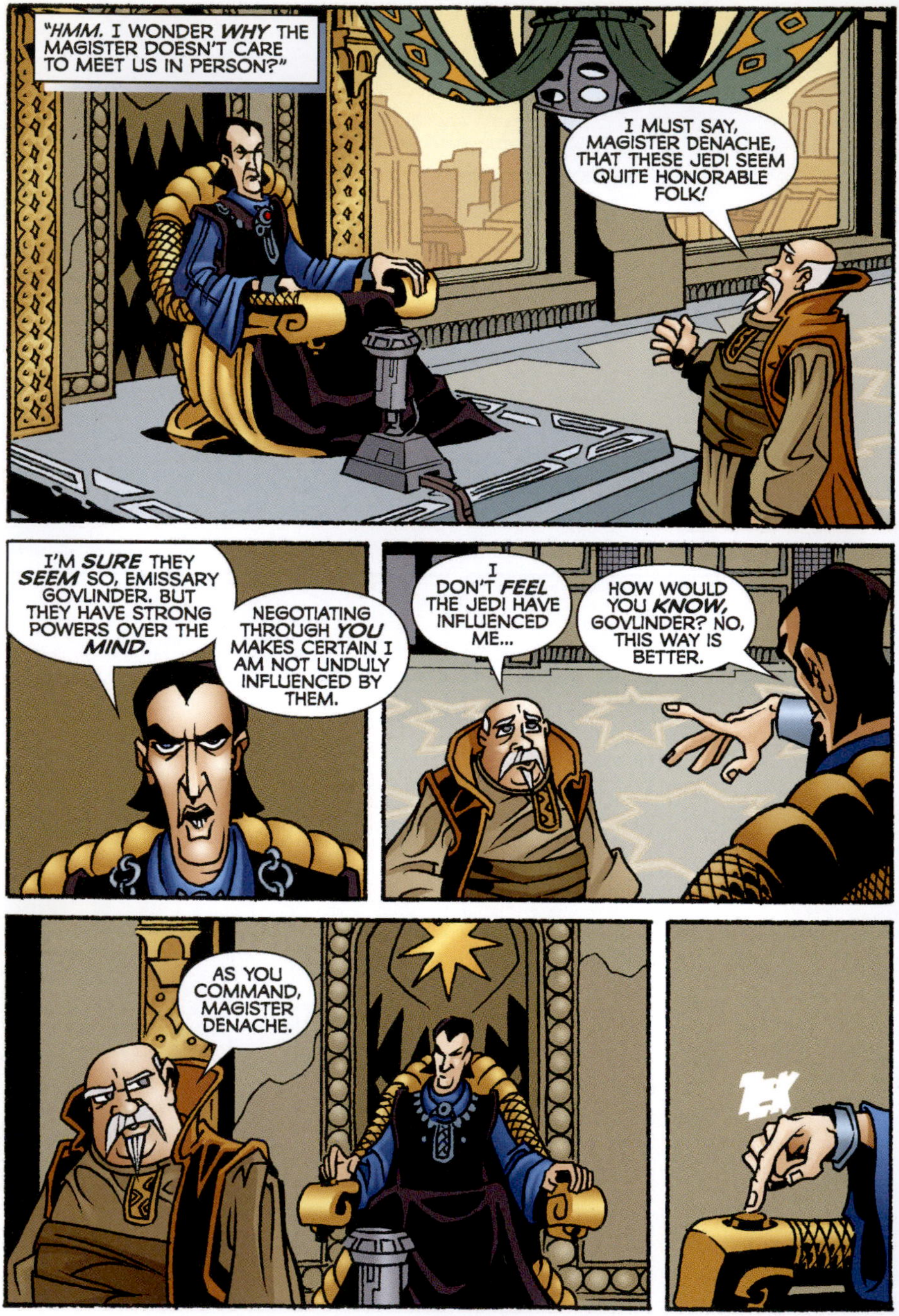
"HMM. I WONDER WHY THE MAGISTER DOESN'T CARE TO MEET US IN PERSON?"
I MUST SAY, MAGISTER DENACHE, THAT THESE JEDI SEEM QUITE HONORABLE FOLK!
I'M SURE THEY SEEM SO, EMISSARY GOVLINDER. BUT THEY HAVE STRONG POWERS OVER THE MIND.
NEGOTIATING THROUGH YOU MAKES CERTAIN I AM NOT UNDULY INFLUENCED BY THEM.
I DON'T FEEL THE JEDI HAVE INFLUENCED ME...
HOW WOULD YOU KNOW, GOVLINDER? NO, THIS WAY IS BETTER.
AS YOU COMMAND, MAGISTER DENACHE.

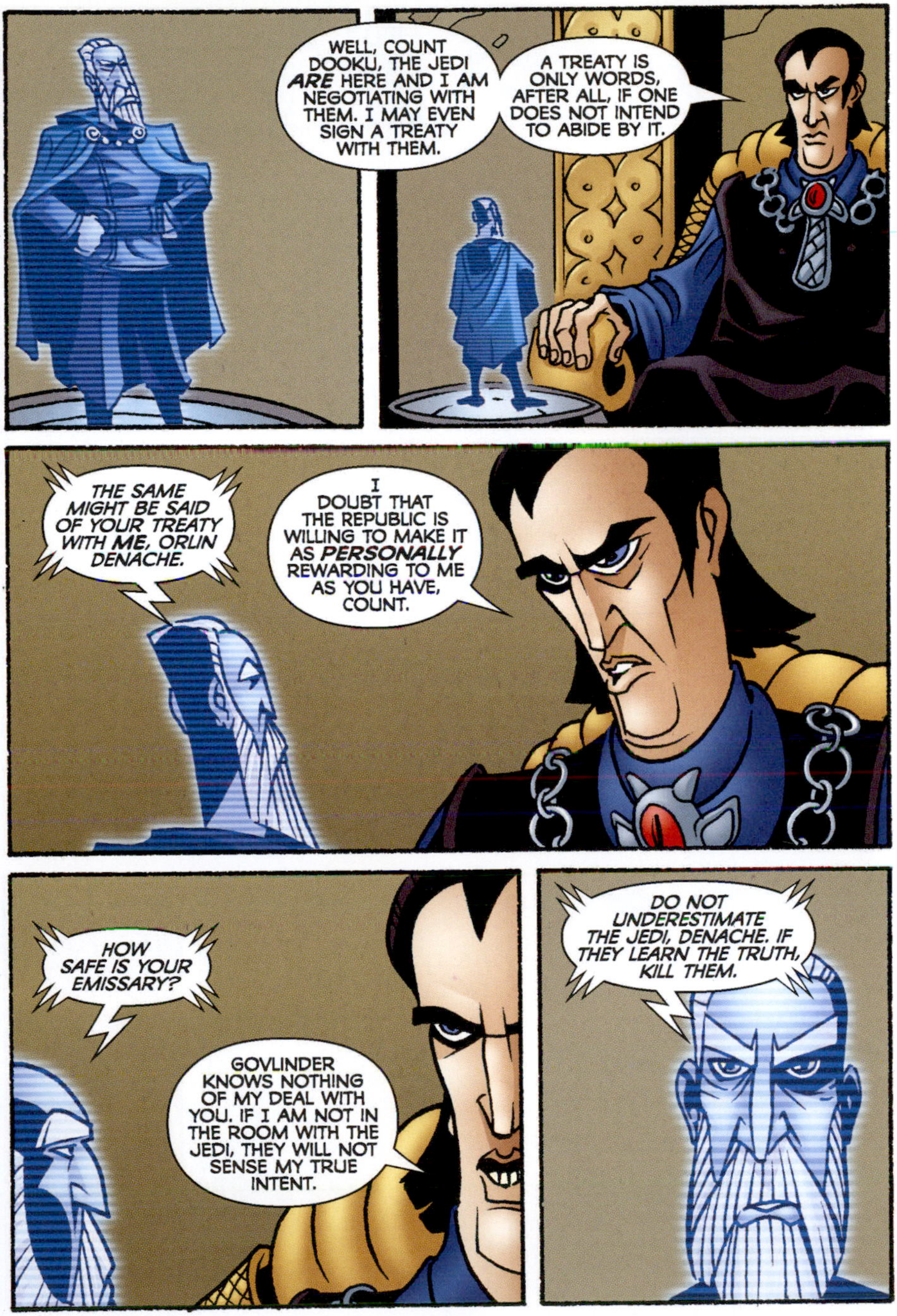
WELL, COUNT DOOKU, THE JEDI ARE HERE AND I AM NEGOTIATING WITH THEM. I MAY EVEN SIGN A TREATY WITH THEM.
A TREATY IS ONLY WORDS, AFTER ALL, IF ONE DOES NOT INTEND TO ABIDE BY IT.
THE SAME MIGHT BE SAID OF YOUR TREATY WITH ME, ORLIN DENACHE.
I DOUBT THAT THE REPUBLIC IS WILLING TO MAKE IT AS PERSONALLY REWARDING TO ME AS YOU HAVE, COUNT.
HOW SAFE IS YOUR EMISSARY?
GOVLINDER KNOWS NOTHING OF MY DEAL WITH YOU. IF I AM NOT IN THE ROOM WITH THE JEDI, THEY WILL NOT SENSE MY TRUE INTENT.
DO NOT UNDERESTIMATE THE JEDI, DENACHE. IF THEY LEARN THE TRUTH, KILL THEM.

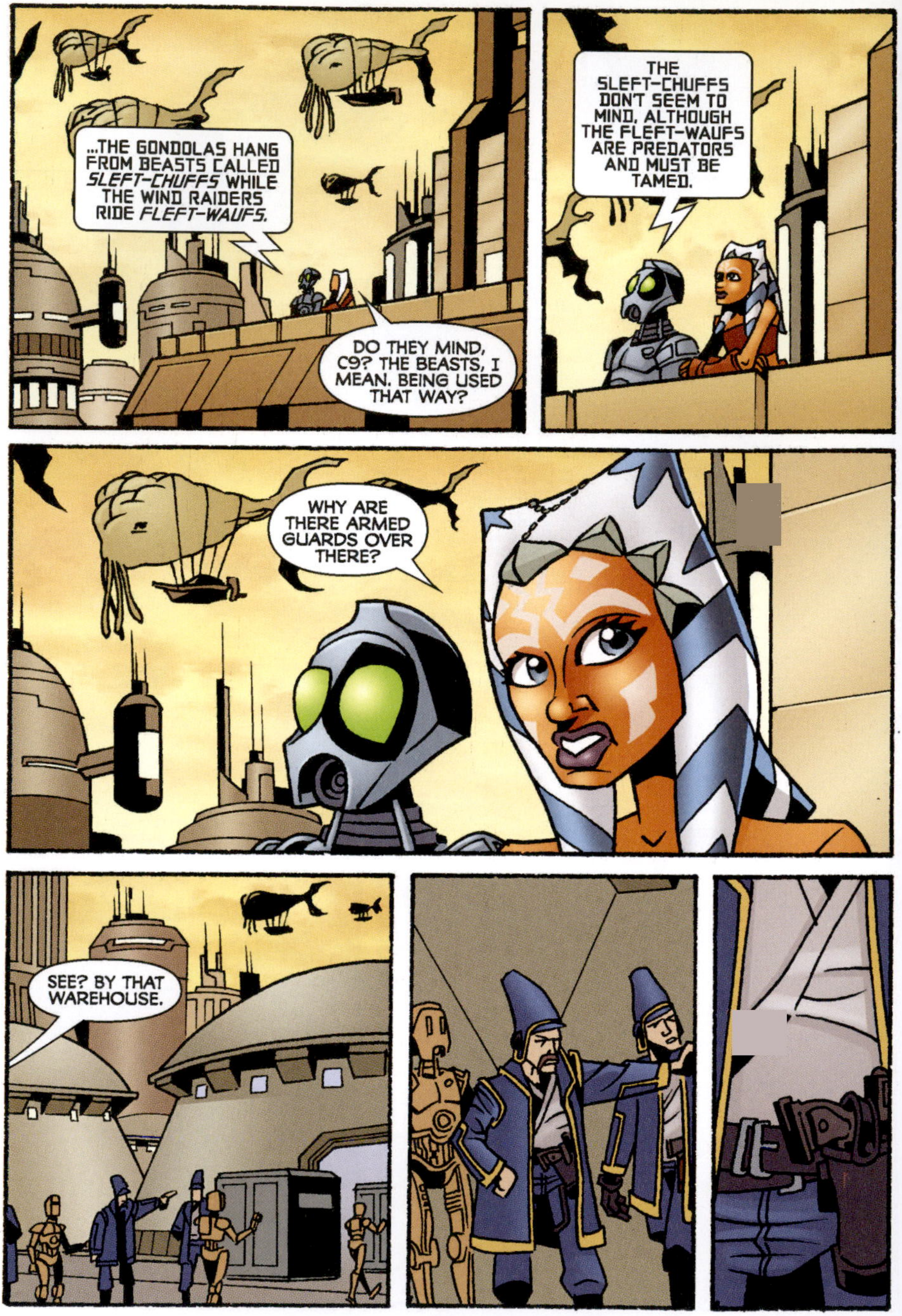
...THE GONDOLAS HANG FROM BEASTS CALLED *SLEFT-CHUFFS* WHILE THE WIND RAIDERS RIDE *FLEFT-WAUFS.*
DO THEY MIND, C9? THE BEASTS, I MEAN. BEING USED THAT WAY?
THE SLEFT-CHUFFS DON'T SEEM TO MIND, ALTHOUGH THE FLEFT-WAUFS ARE PREDATORS AND MUST BE TAMED.
WHY ARE THERE ARMED GUARDS OVER THERE?
SEE? BY THAT WAREHOUSE.

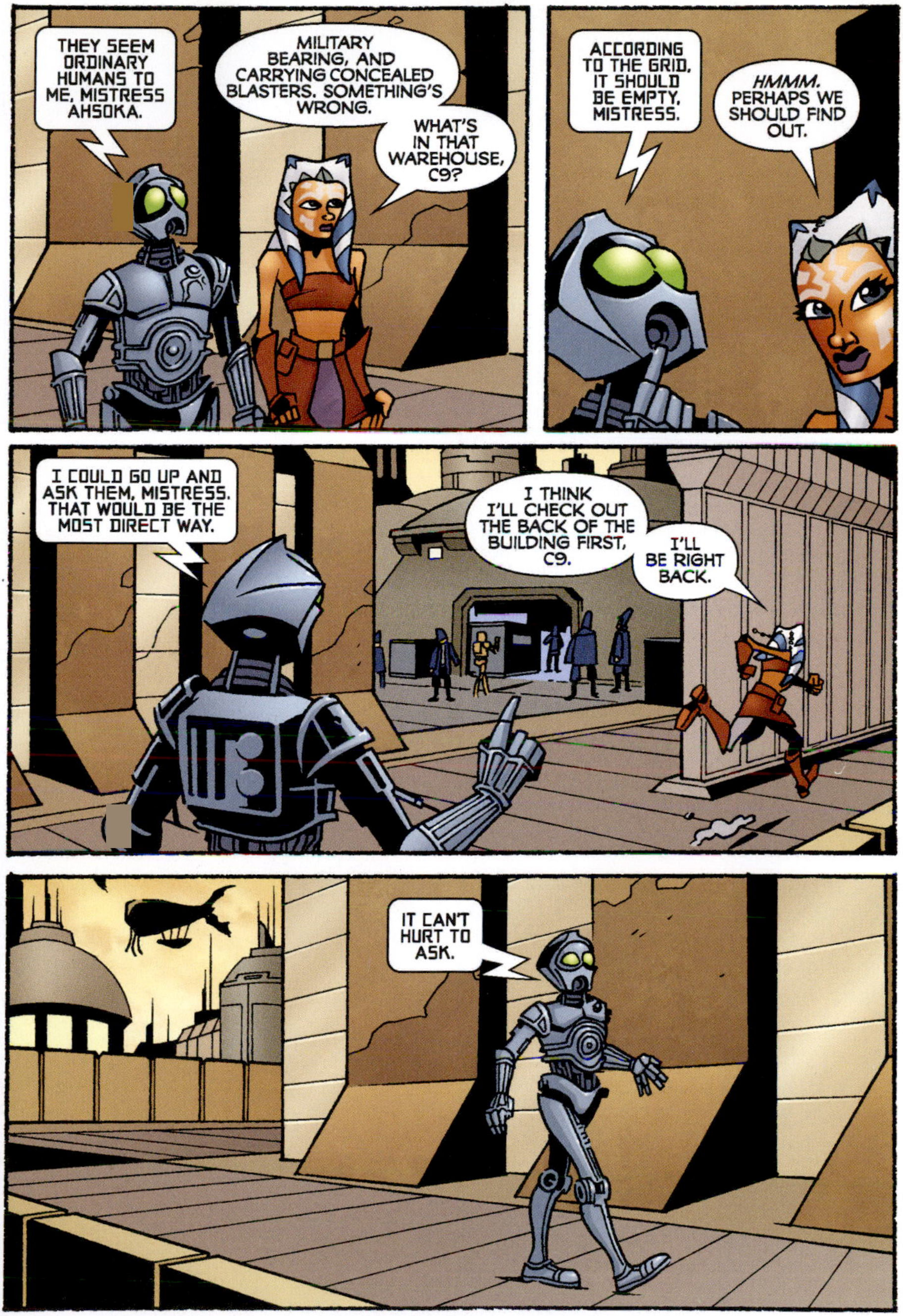
THEY SEEM ORDINARY HUMANS TO ME, MISTRESS AHSOKA.
MILITARY BEARING, AND CARRYING CONCEALED BLASTERS. SOMETHING'S WRONG.
WHAT'S IN THAT WAREHOUSE, C9?
ACCORDING TO THE GRID, IT SHOULD BE EMPTY, MISTRESS.
HMMM. PERHAPS WE SHOULD FIND OUT.
I COULD GO UP AND ASK THEM, MISTRESS. THAT WOULD BE THE MOST DIRECT WAY.
I THINK I'LL CHECK OUT THE BACK OF THE BUILDING FIRST, C9.
I'LL BE RIGHT BACK.
IT CAN'T HURT TO ASK.

IN THE ALLEY BEHIND THE WAREHOUSE...

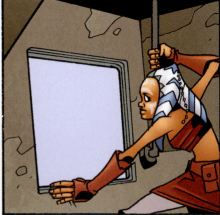

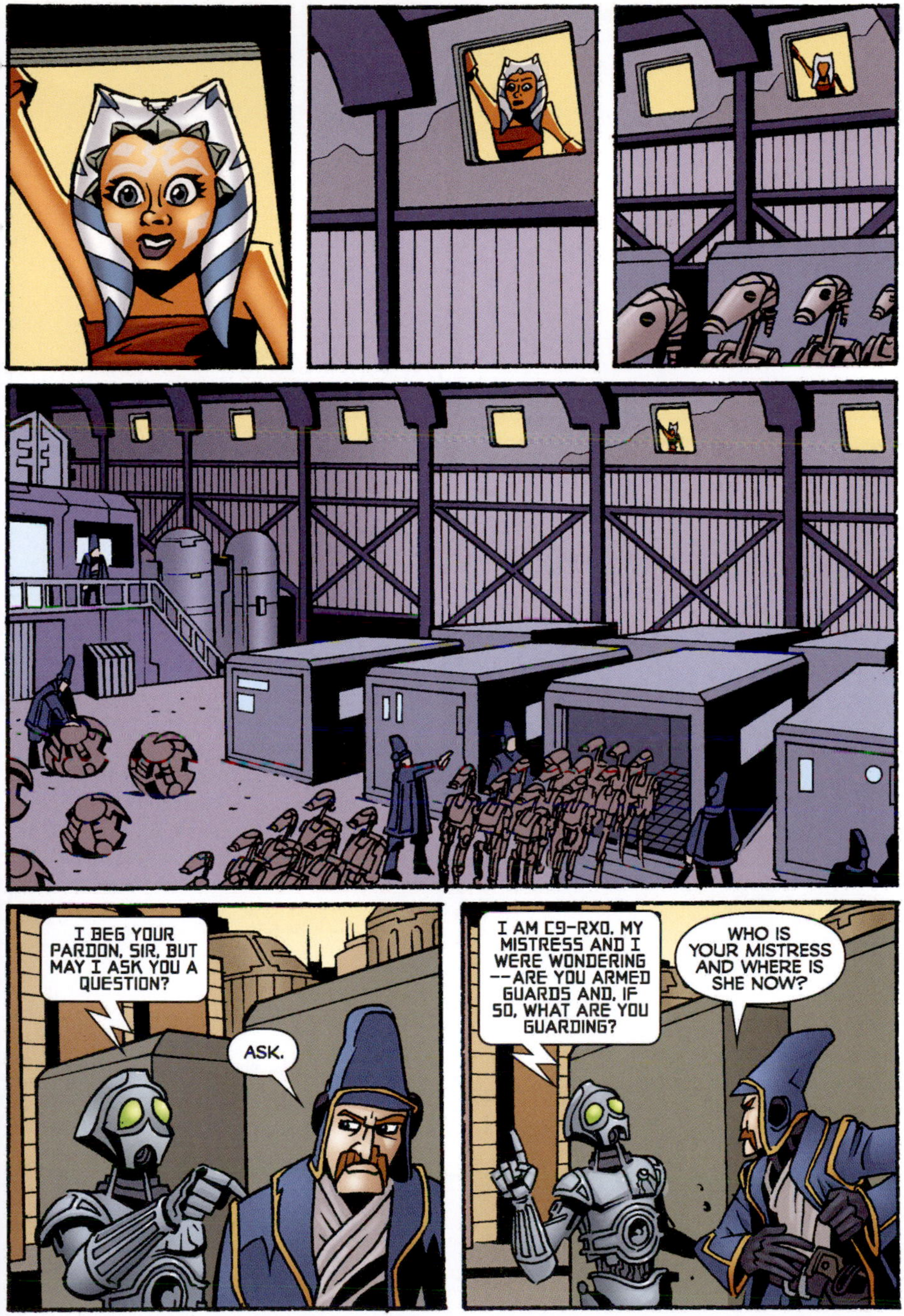

I BEG YOUR PARDON, SIR, BUT MAY I ASK YOU A QUESTION?
ASK.
I AM C9-RX0. MY MISTRESS AND I WERE WONDERING --ARE YOU ARMED GUARDS AND, IF SO, WHAT ARE YOU GUARDING?
WHO IS YOUR MISTRESS AND WHERE IS SHE NOW?

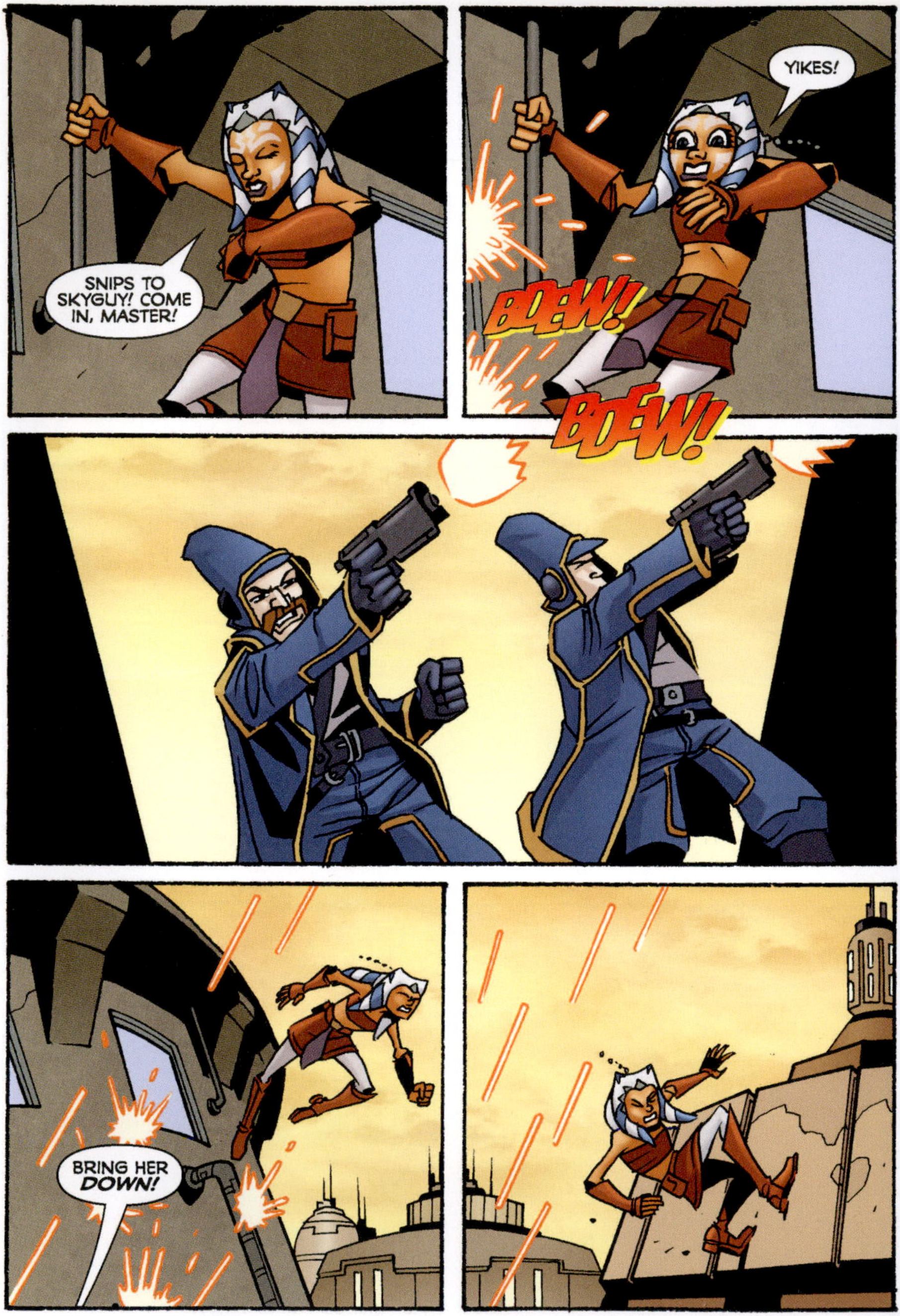
SNIPS TO SKYGUY! COME IN, MASTER!
YIKES!
BDEW!
BDEW!
BRING HER DOWN!

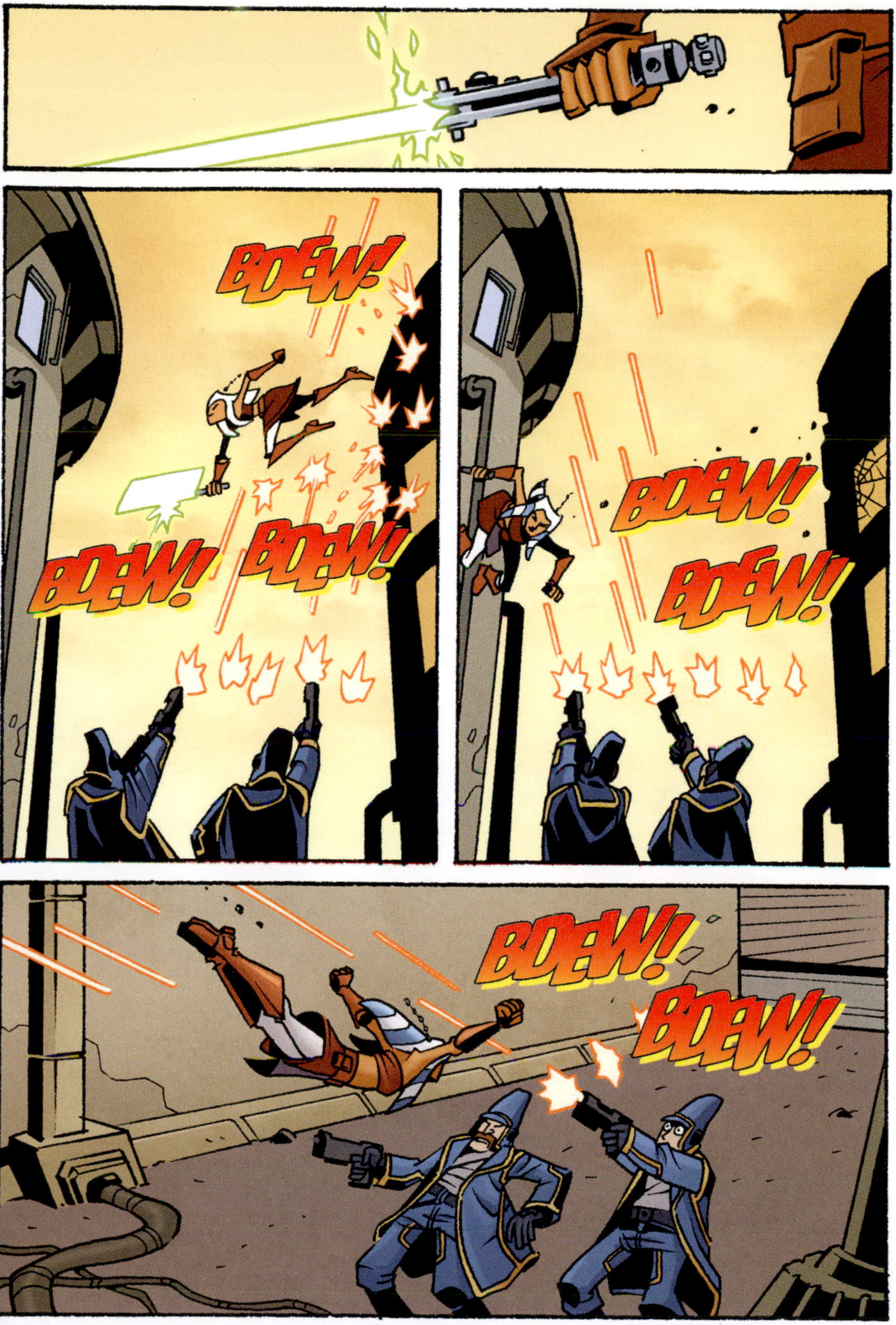
BDEW!
BDEW!
BDEW!
BDEW!
BDEW!
BDEW!
BDEW!

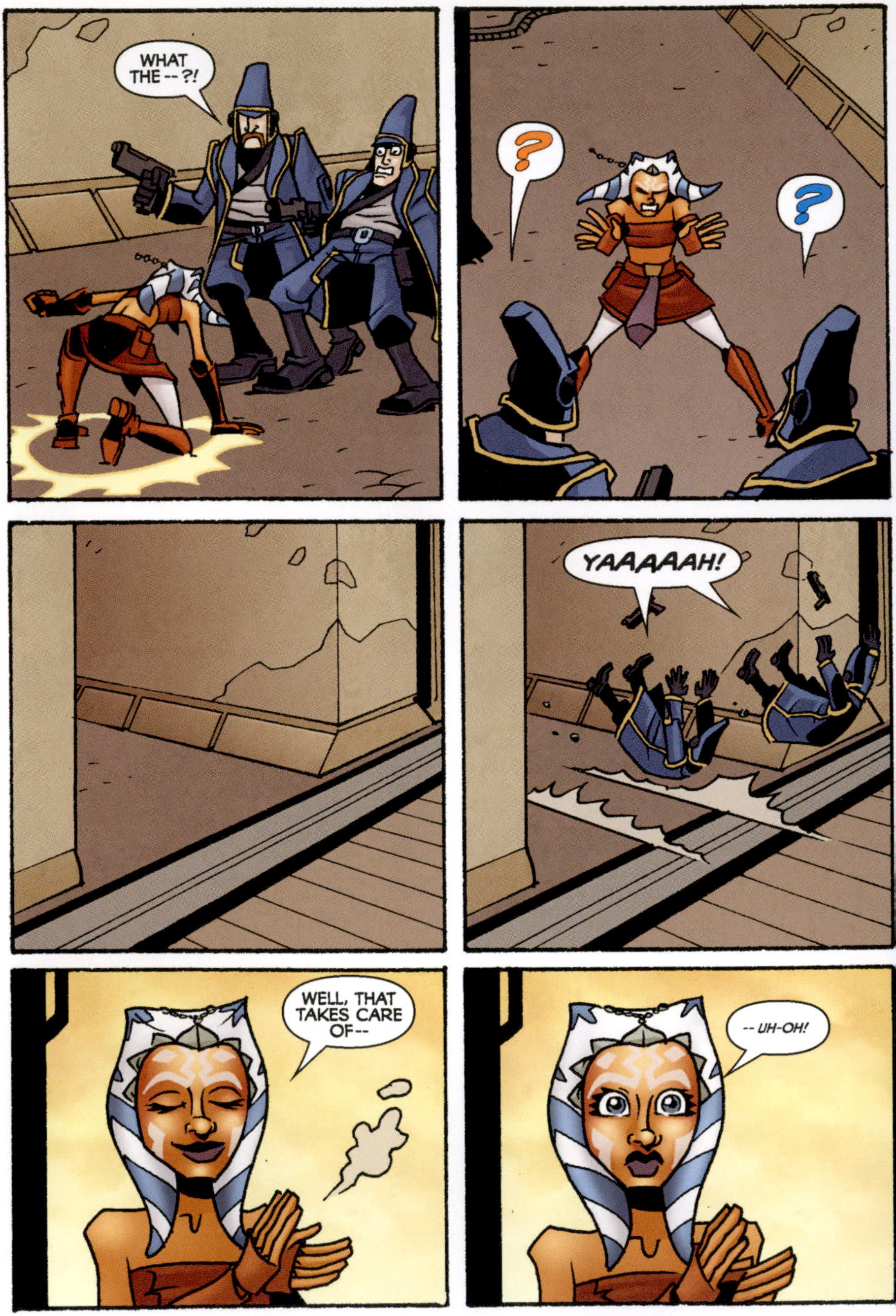
WHAT THE--?!
?
?
YAAAAAH!
WELL, THAT TAKES CARE OF--
--UH-OH!

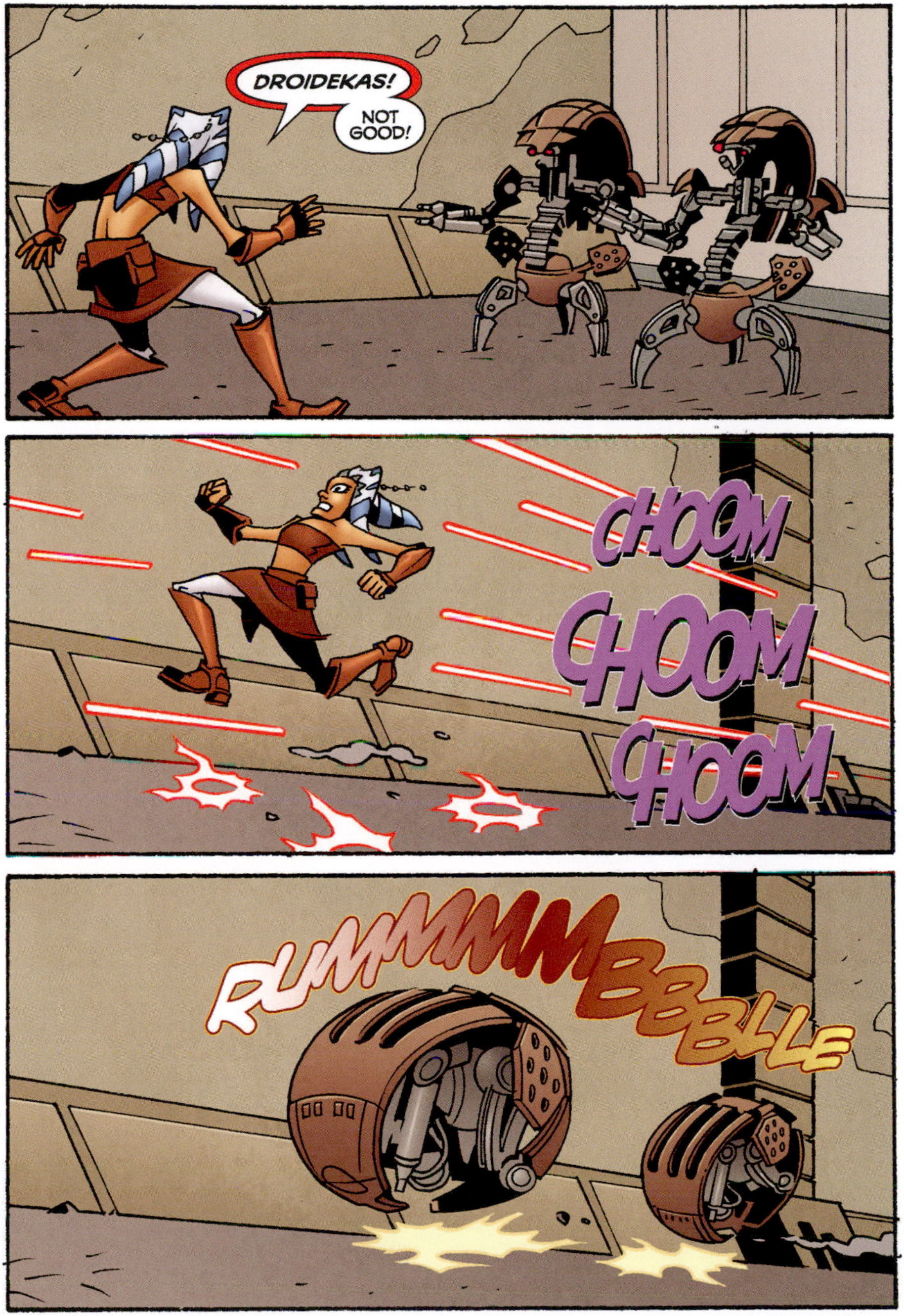
DROIDEKAS!
NOT GOOD!
CHOOM
CHOOM
CHOOM
RUMMMMMBBBLLE

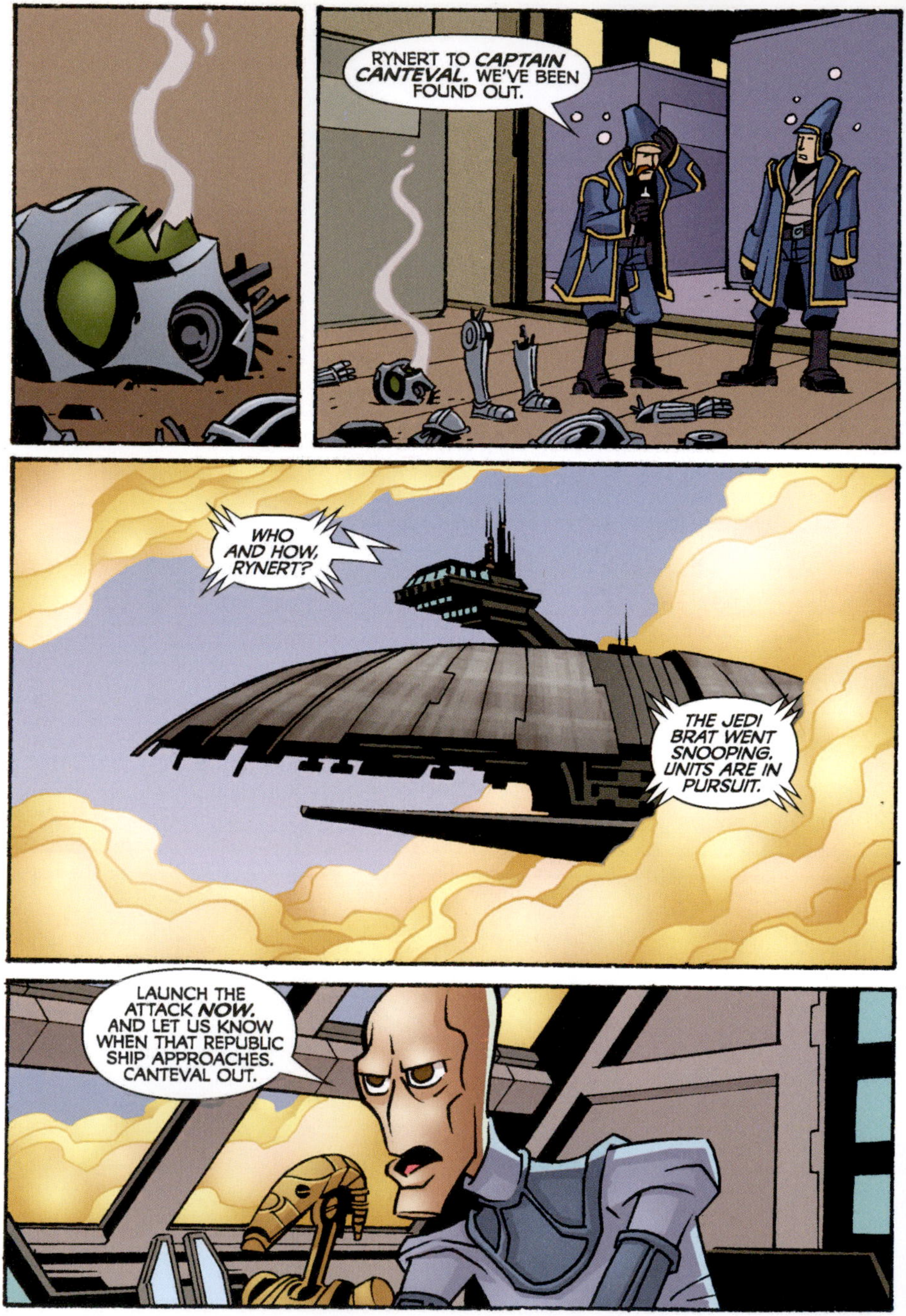
RYNERT TO CAPTAIN CANTEVAL. WE'VE BEEN FOUND OUT.
WHO AND HOW, RYNERT?
THE JEDI BRAT WENT SNOOPING. UNITS ARE IN PURSUIT.
LAUNCH THE ATTACK NOW. AND LET US KNOW WHEN THAT REPUBLIC SHIP APPROACHES. CANTEVAL OUT.

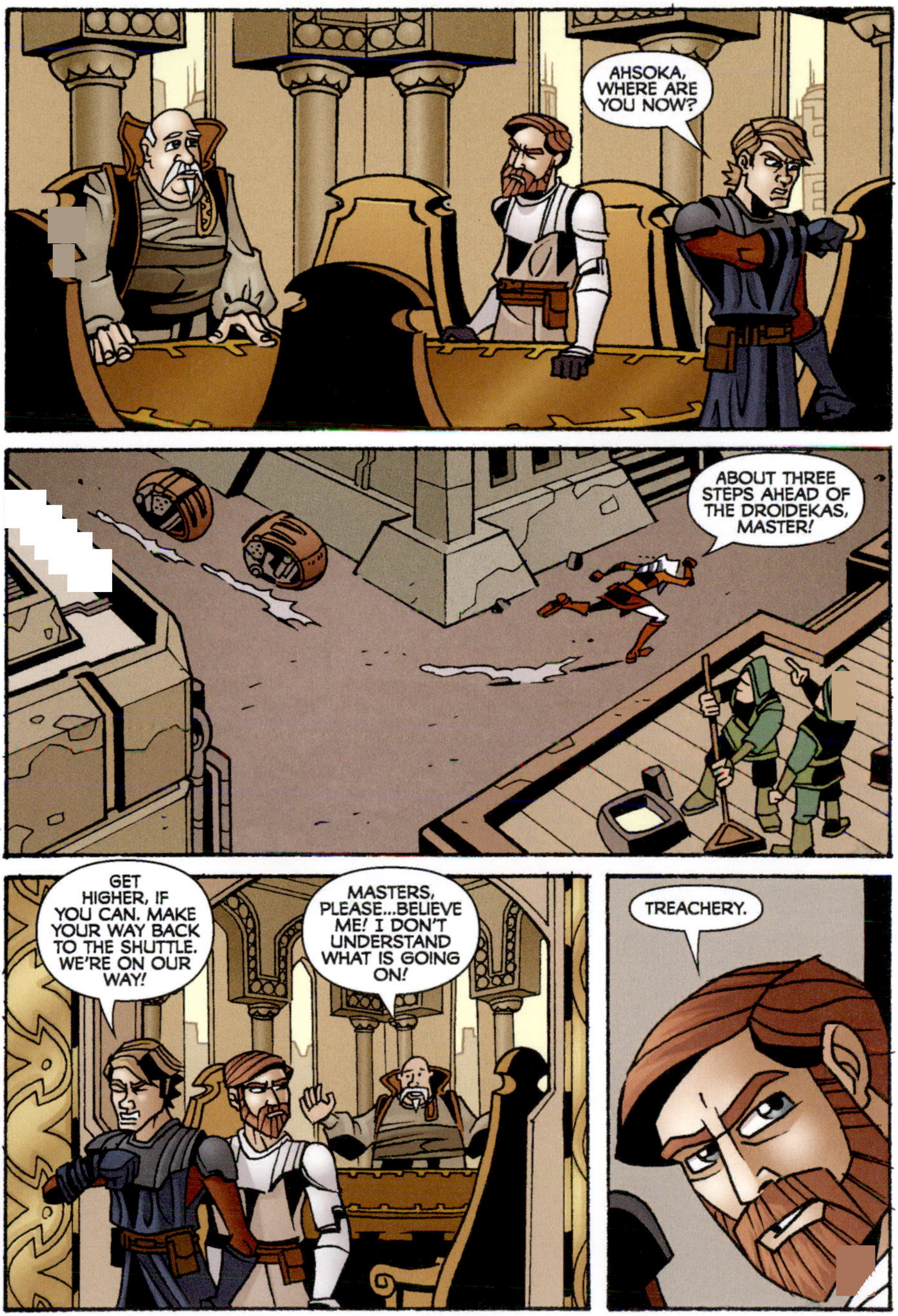
AHSOKA, WHERE ARE YOU NOW?
ABOUT THREE STEPS AHEAD OF THE DROIDEKAS, MASTER!
GET HIGHER, IF YOU CAN. MAKE YOUR WAY BACK TO THE SHUTTLE. WE'RE ON OUR WAY!
MASTERS, PLEASE...BELIEVE ME! I DON'T UNDERSTAND WHAT IS GOING ON!
TREACHERY.

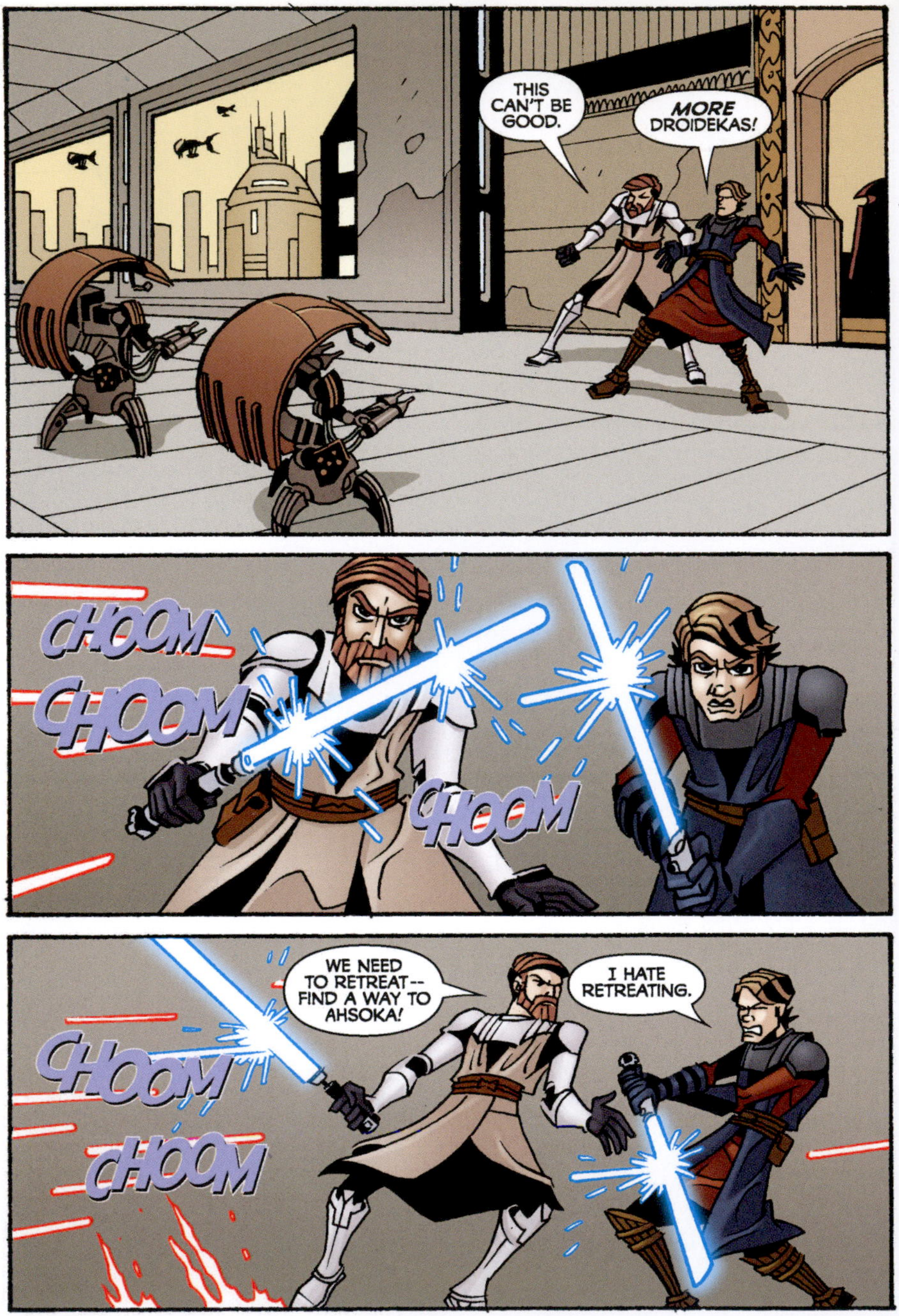
THIS CAN'T BE GOOD.
MORE DROIDEKAS!
CHOOM
CHOOM
CHOOM
CHOOM
CHOOM
WE NEED TO RETREAT-- FIND A WAY TO AHSOKA!
I HATE RETREATING.

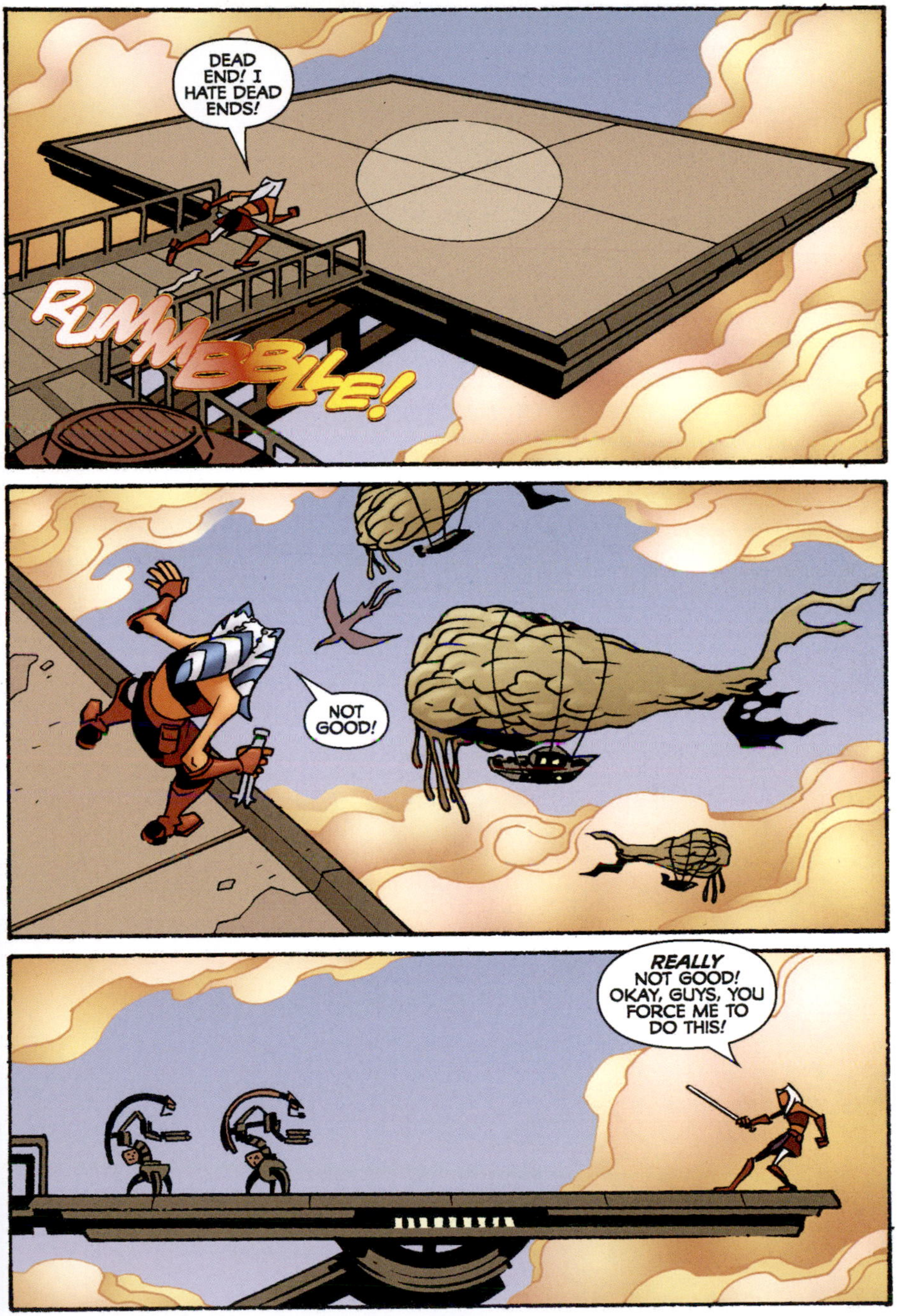
DEAD END! I HATE DEAD ENDS!
RUMMBBLLE!
NOT GOOD!
REALLY NOT GOOD! OKAY, GUYS, YOU FORCE ME TO DO THIS!

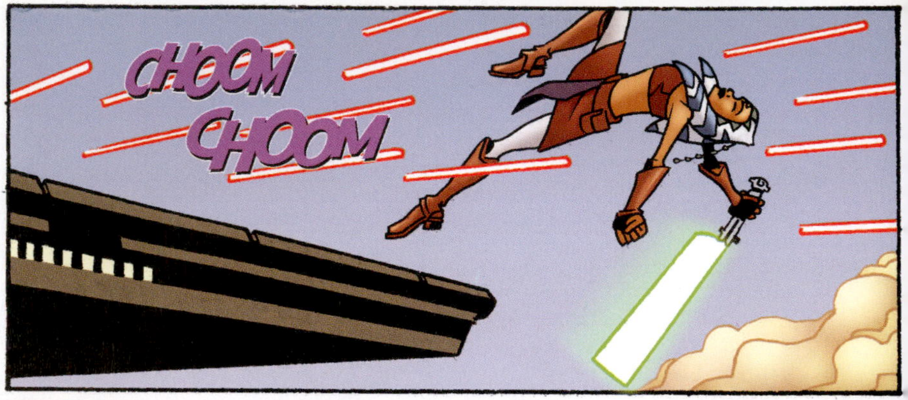
CHOOM
CHOOM

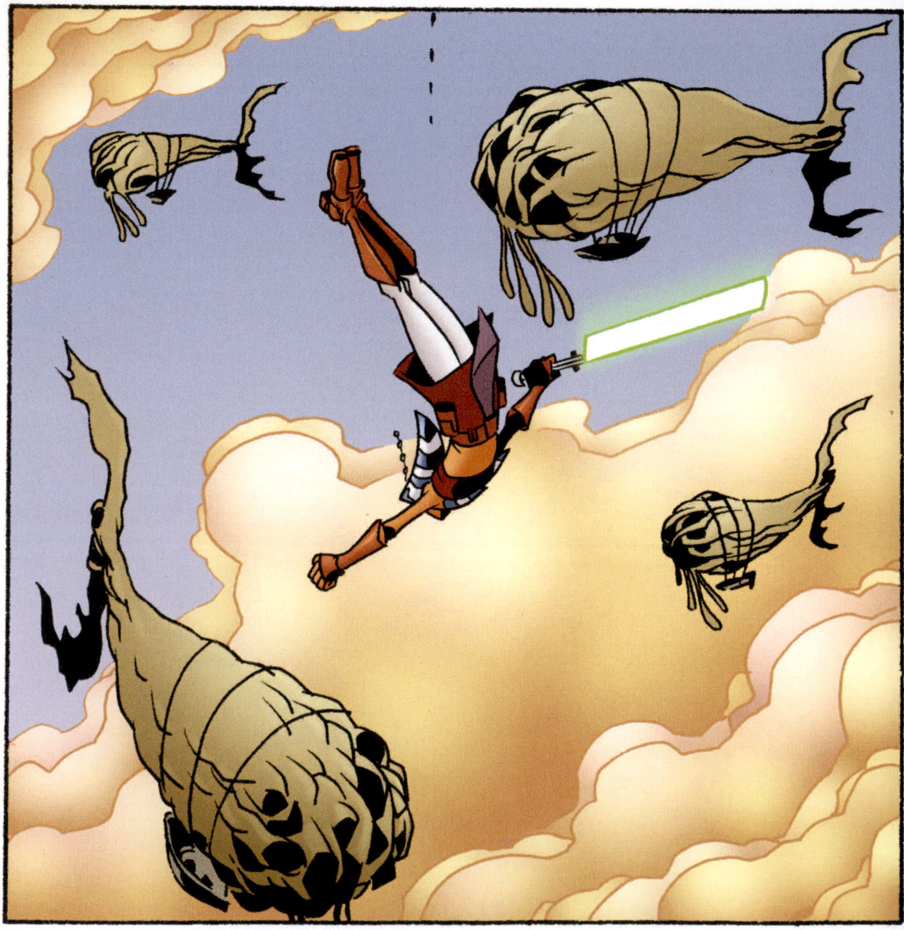

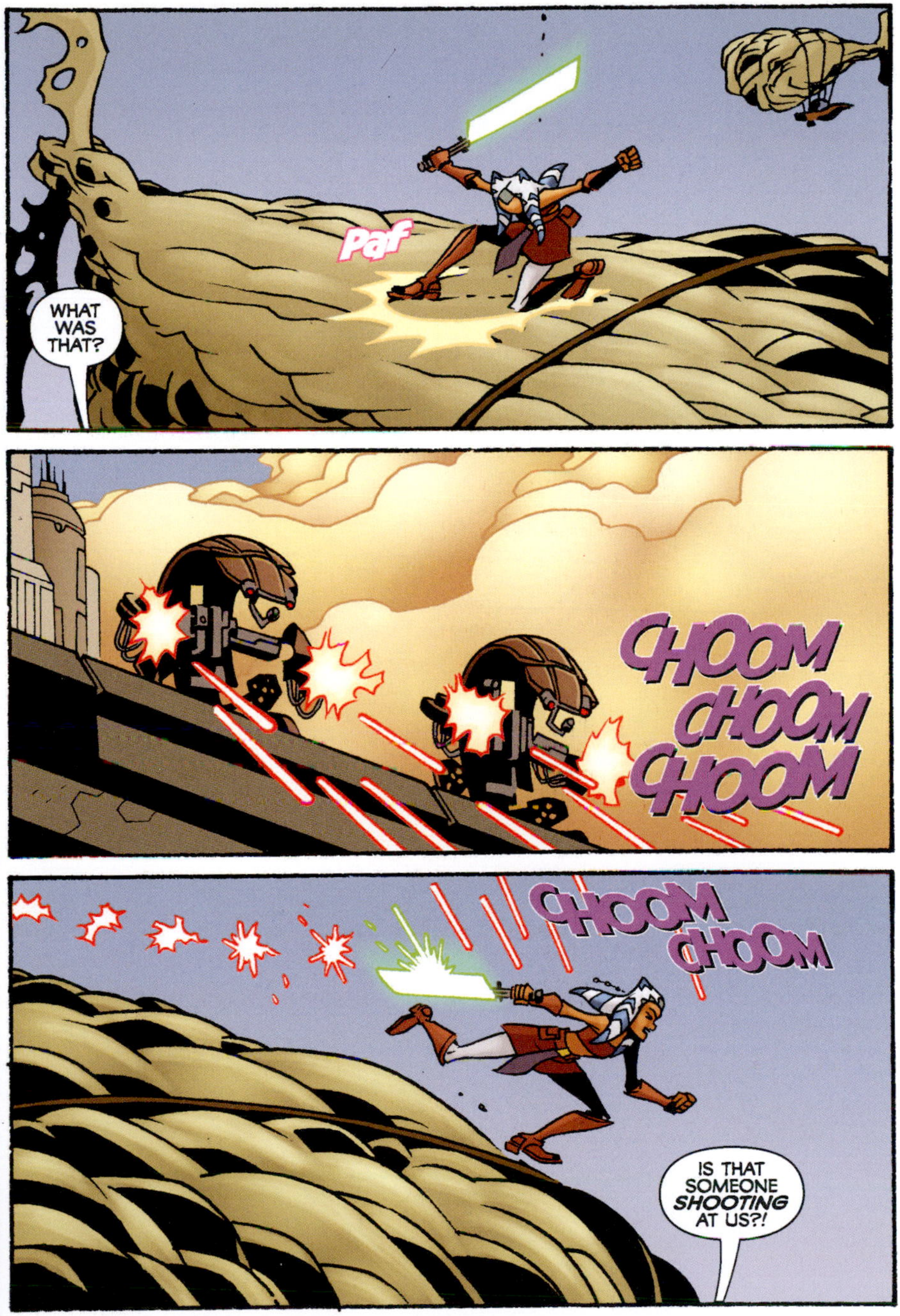
Paf
WHAT WAS THAT?
CHOOM
CHOOM
CHOOM
CHOOM
CHOOM
IS THAT SOMEONE *SHOOTING* AT US?!

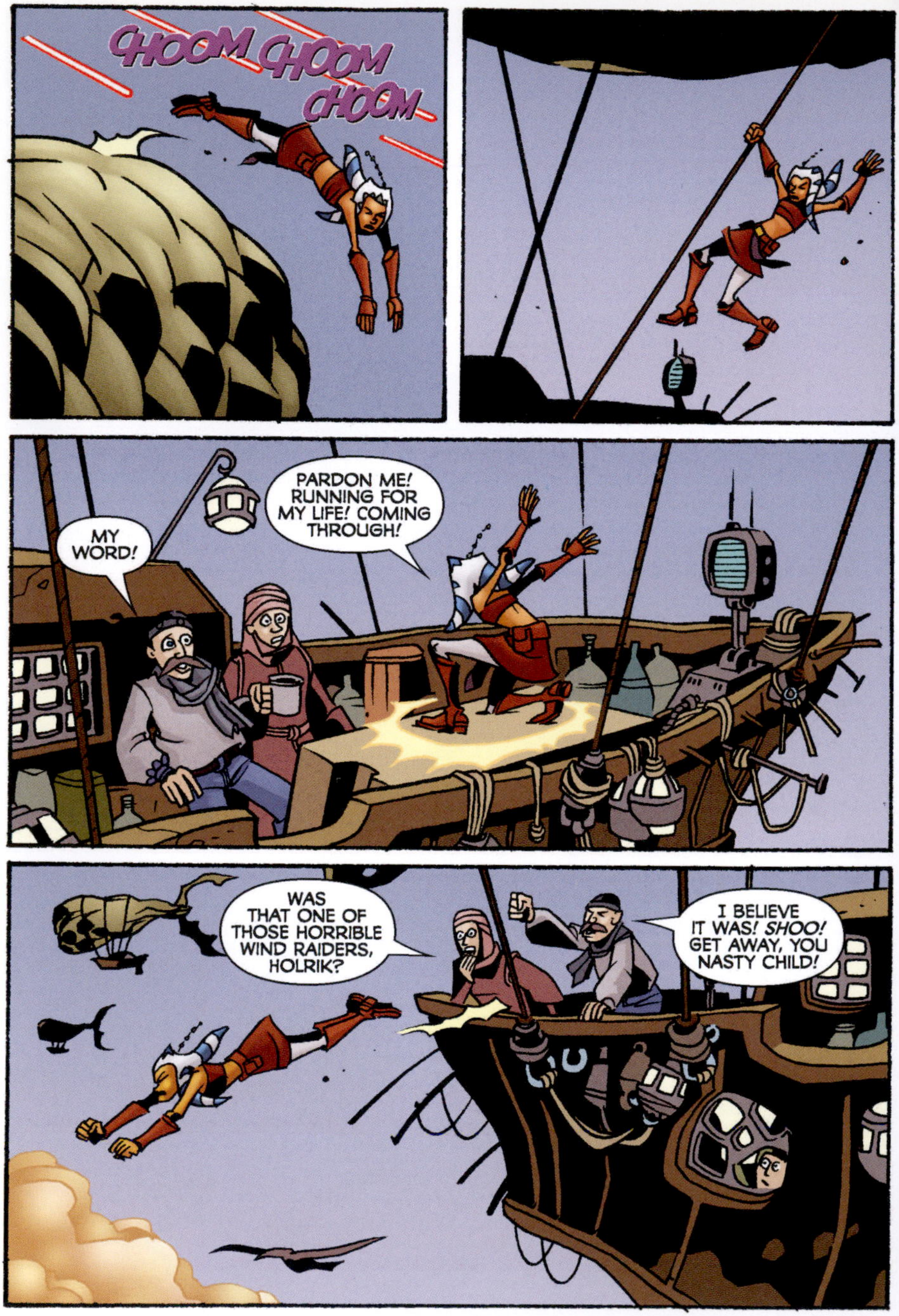
CHOOM CHOOM CHOOM
MY WORD!
PARDON ME! RUNNING FOR MY LIFE! COMING THROUGH!
WAS THAT ONE OF THOSE HORRIBLE WIND RAIDERS, HOLRIK?
I BELIEVE IT WAS! *SHOO!* GET AWAY, YOU NASTY CHILD!

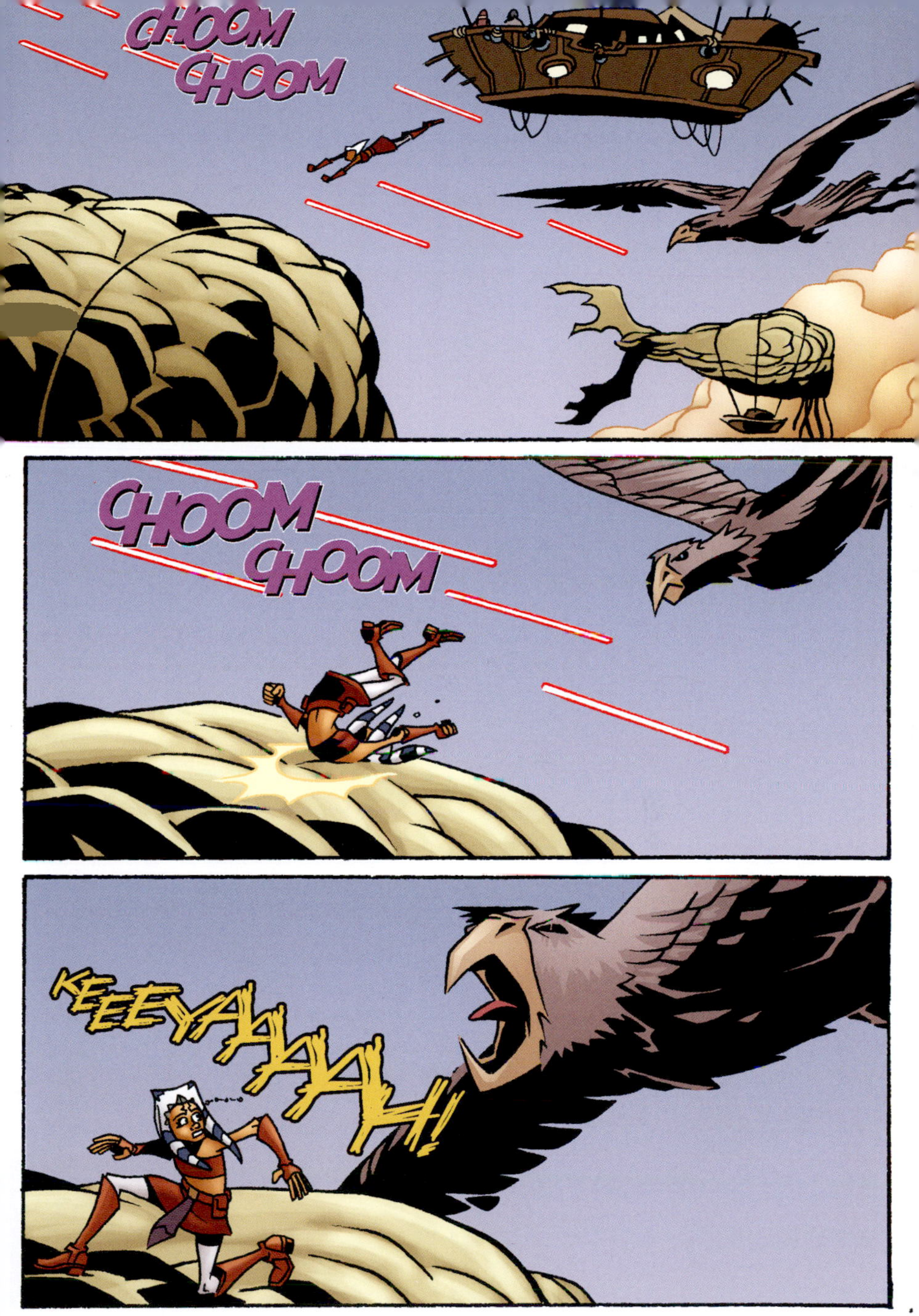
CHOOM CHOOM
CHOOM CHOOM
KEEEYAAAAH!

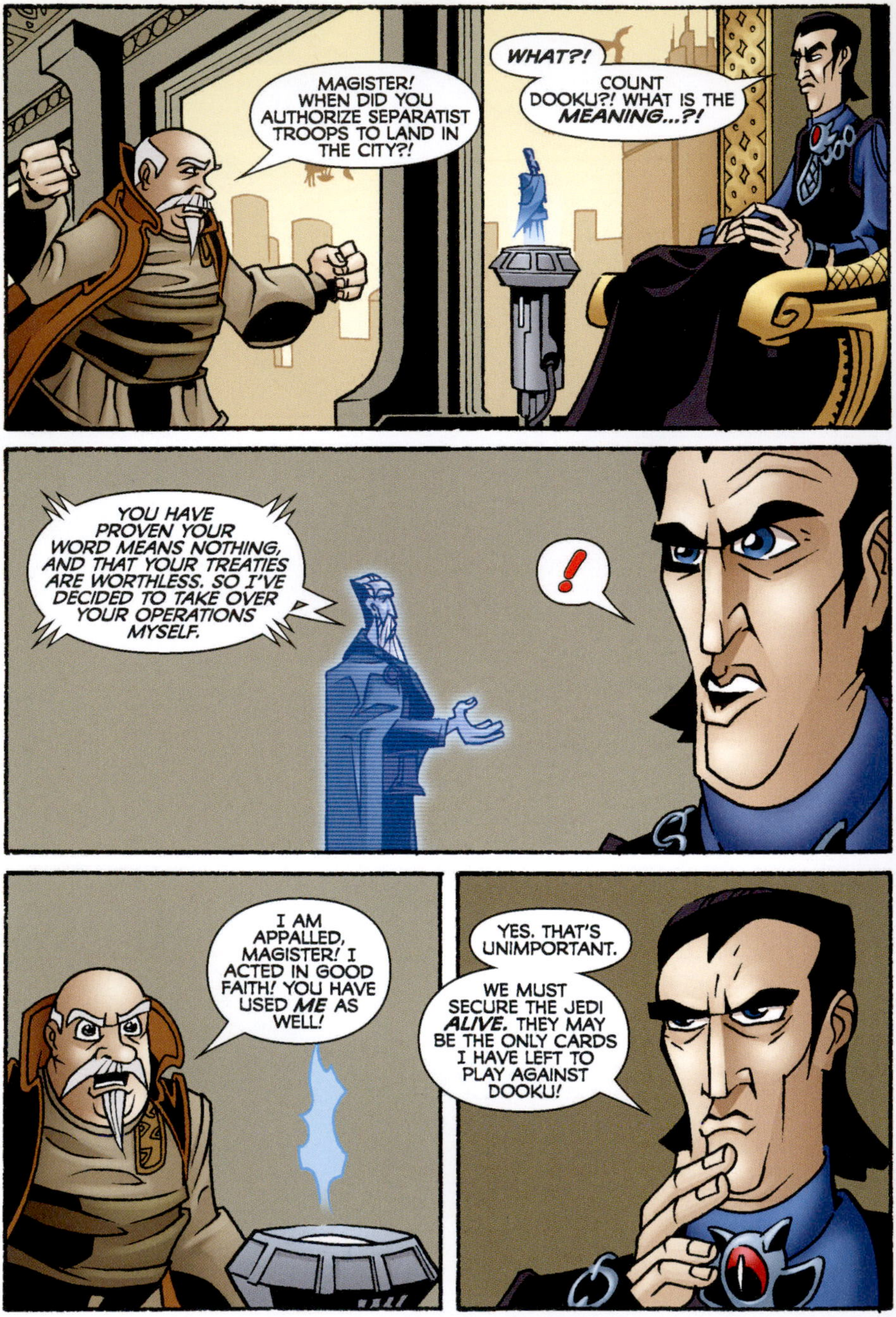
MAGISTER! WHEN DID YOU AUTHORIZE SEPARATIST TROOPS TO LAND IN THE CITY?!
WHAT?!
COUNT DOOKU?! WHAT IS THE MEANING...?!
YOU HAVE PROVEN YOUR WORD MEANS NOTHING, AND THAT YOUR TREATIES ARE WORTHLESS. SO I'VE DECIDED TO TAKE OVER YOUR OPERATIONS MYSELF.
!
I AM APPALLED, MAGISTER! I ACTED IN GOOD FAITH! YOU HAVE USED ME AS WELL!
YES. THAT'S UNIMPORTANT.
WE MUST SECURE THE JEDI ALIVE. THEY MAY BE THE ONLY CARDS I HAVE LEFT TO PLAY AGAINST DOOKU!

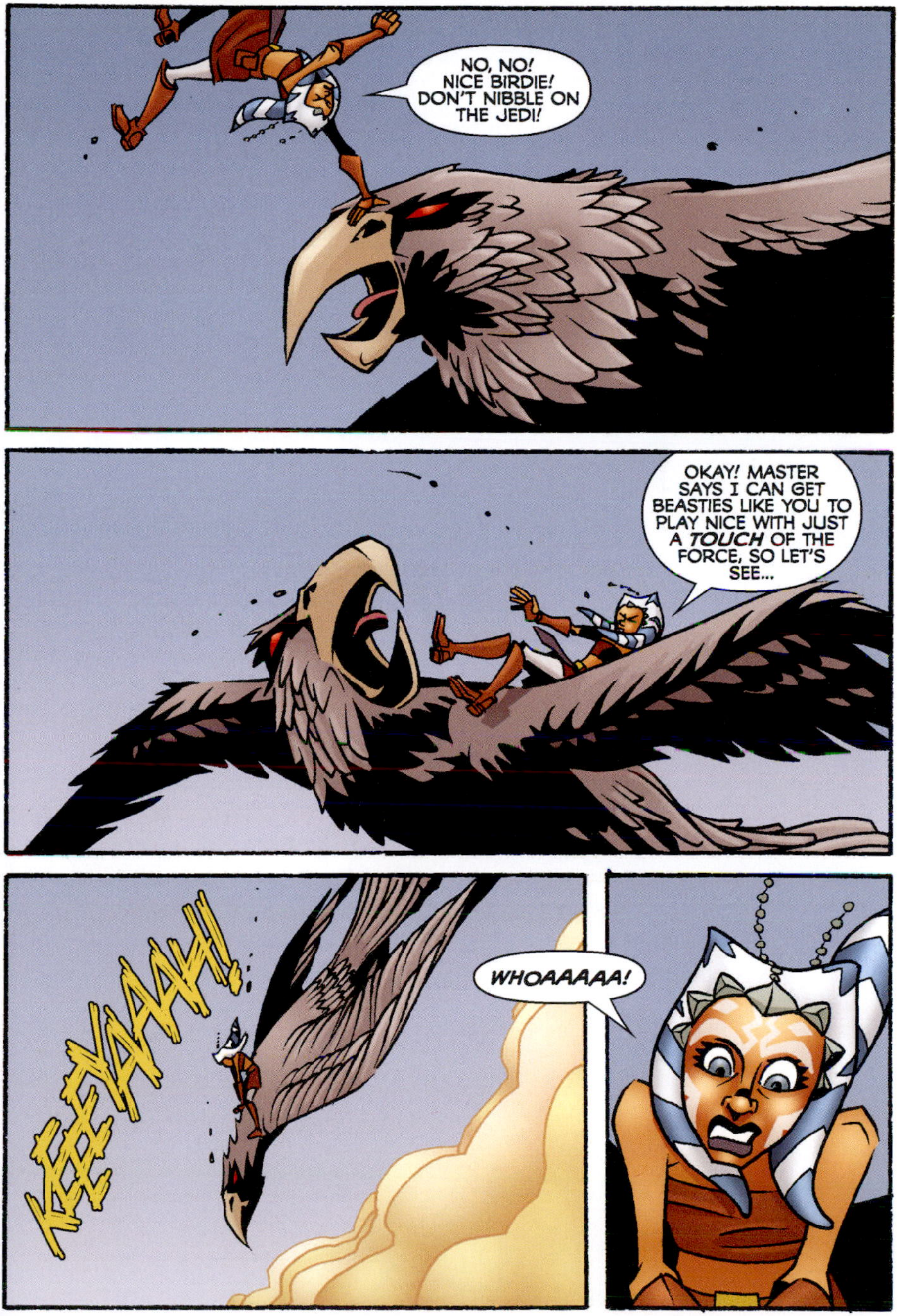
NO, NO! NICE BIRDIE! DON'T NIBBLE ON THE JEDI!
OKAY! MASTER SAYS I CAN GET BEASTIES LIKE YOU TO PLAY NICE WITH JUST A *TOUCH* OF THE FORCE, SO LET'S SEE...
KREEYAAAH!
WHOAAAAAA!

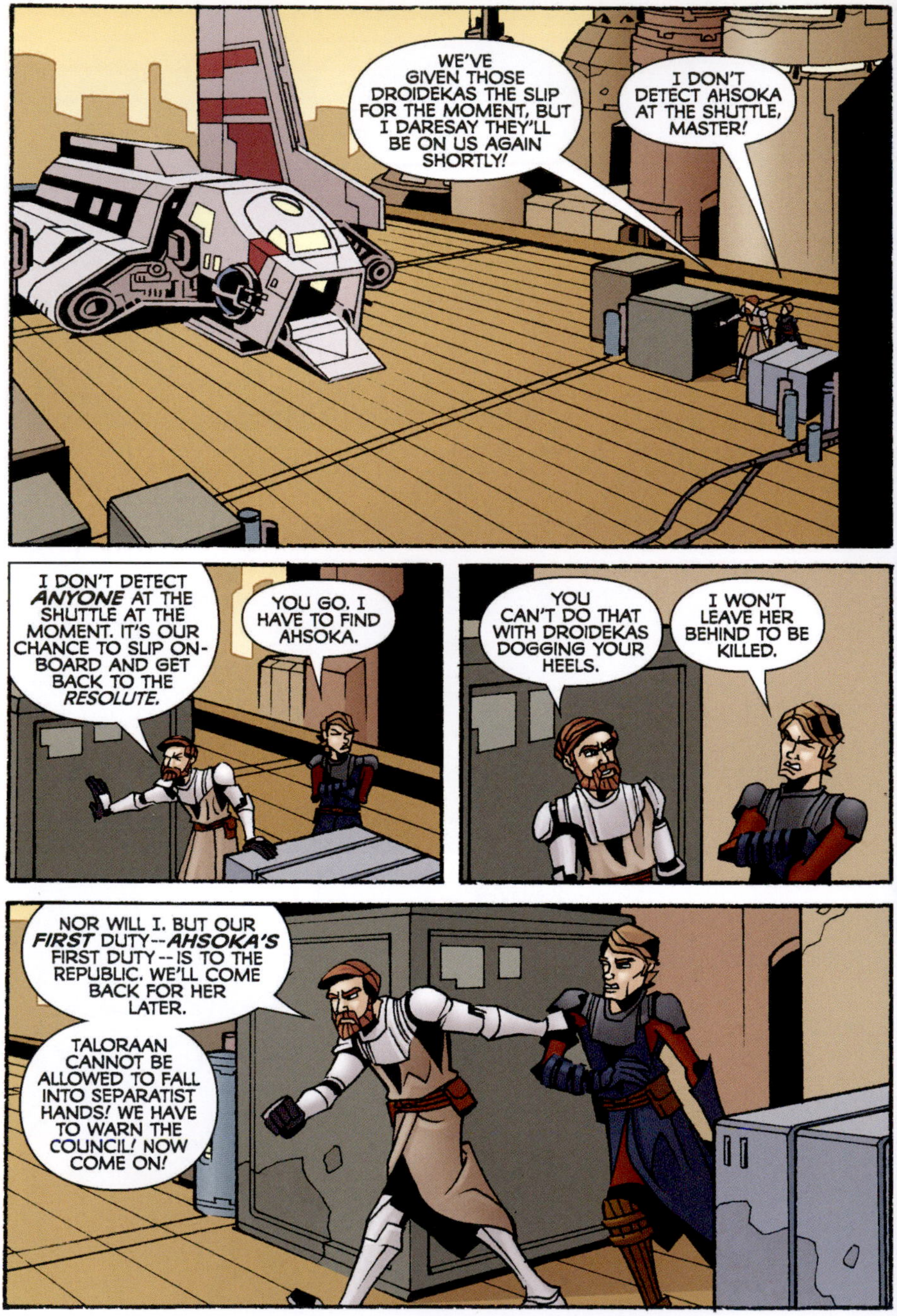

WE'VE GIVEN THOSE DROIDEKAS THE SLIP FOR THE MOMENT, BUT I DARESAY THEY'LL BE ON US AGAIN SHORTLY!
I DON'T DETECT AHSOKA AT THE SHUTTLE, MASTER!
I DON'T DETECT *ANYONE* AT THE SHUTTLE AT THE MOMENT. IT'S OUR CHANCE TO SLIP ON-BOARD AND GET BACK TO THE *RESOLUTE.*
YOU GO. I HAVE TO FIND AHSOKA.
YOU CAN'T DO THAT WITH DROIDEKAS DOGGING YOUR HEELS.
I WON'T LEAVE HER BEHIND TO BE KILLED.
NOR WILL I. BUT OUR *FIRST* DUTY--*AHSOKA'S* FIRST DUTY--IS TO THE REPUBLIC. WE'LL COME BACK FOR HER LATER.
TALORAAN CANNOT BE ALLOWED TO FALL INTO SEPARATIST HANDS! WE HAVE TO WARN THE COUNCIL! NOW COME ON!

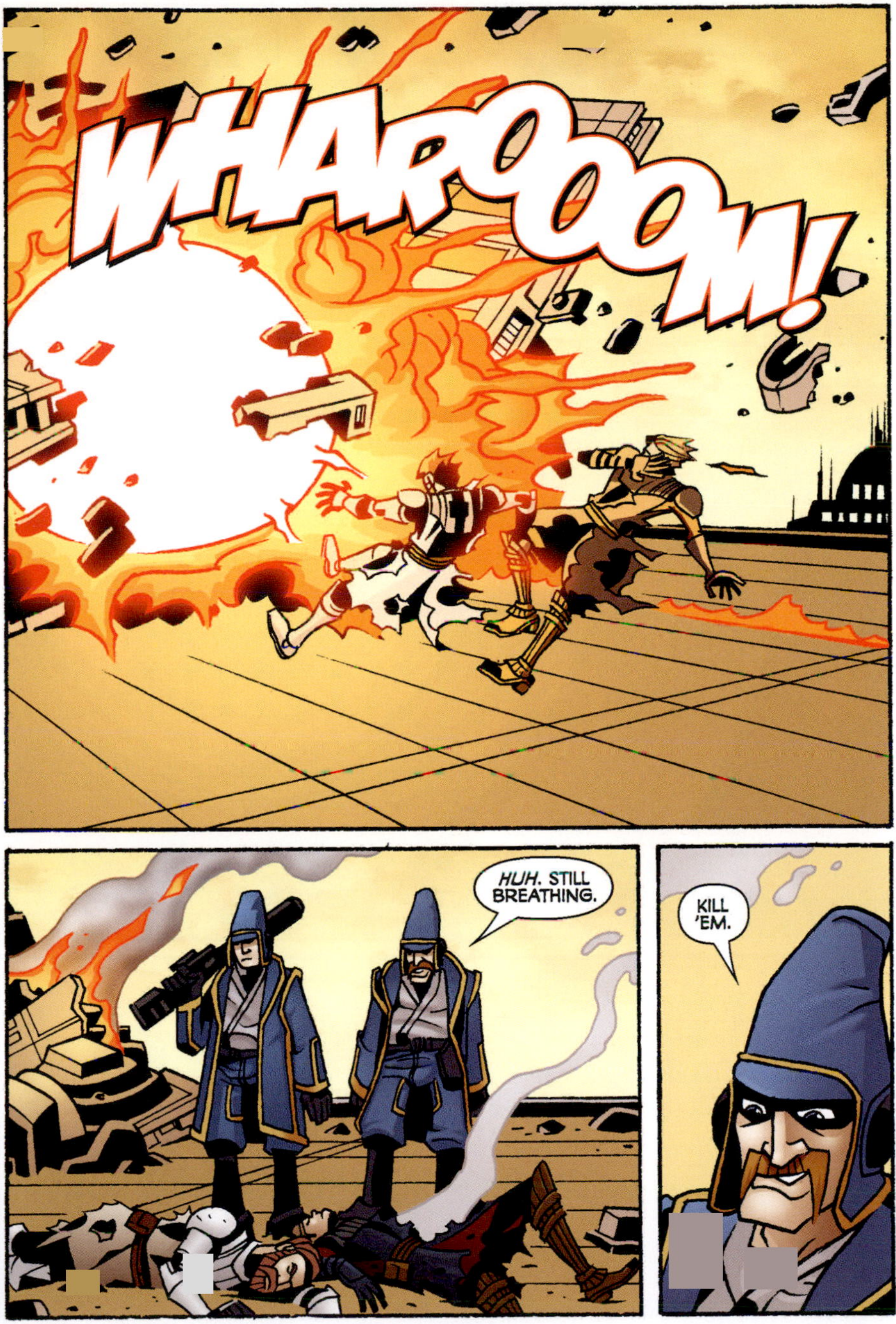
WHAROOOM!
HUH. STILL BREATHING.
KILL 'EM.

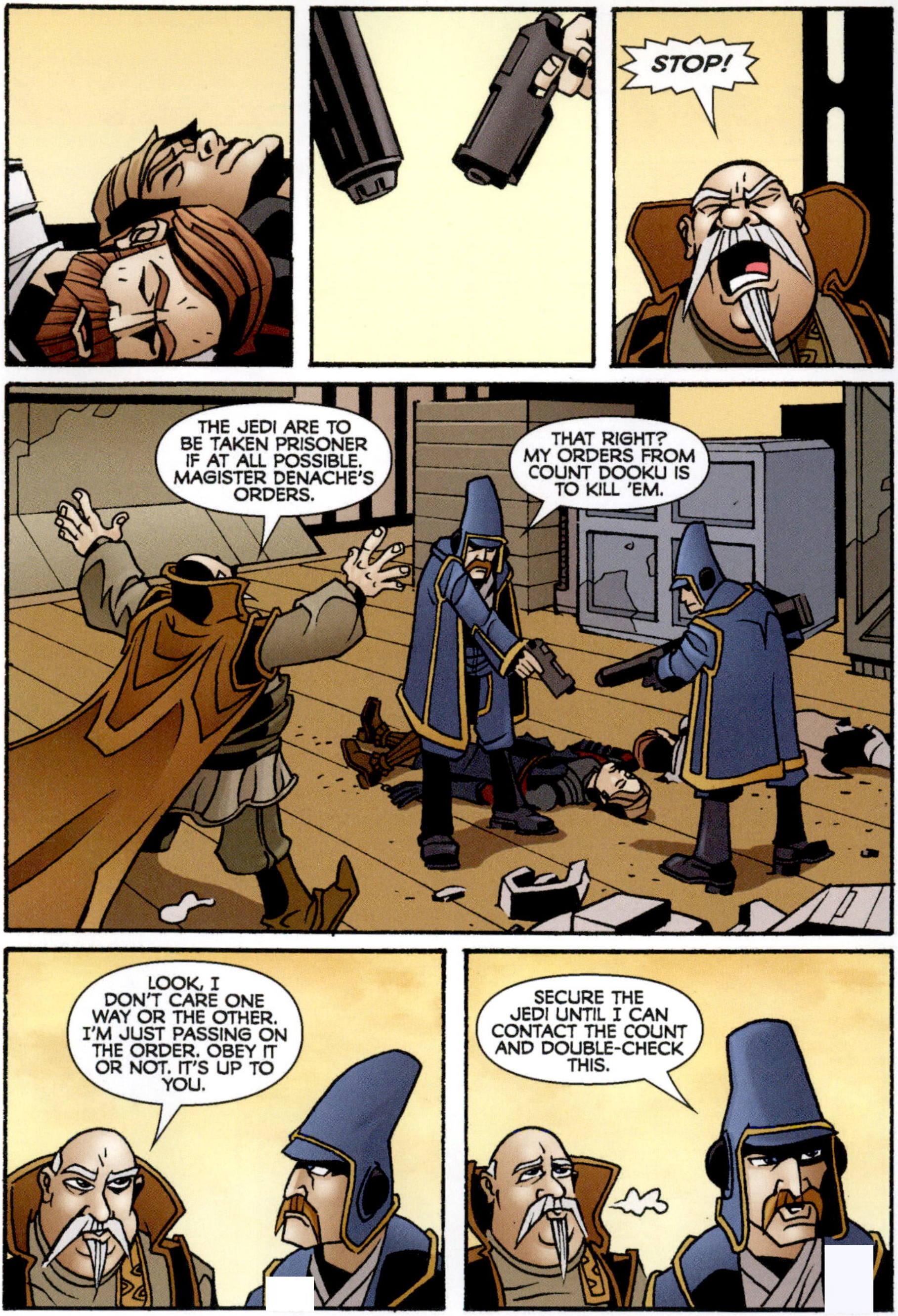
STOP!
THE JEDI ARE TO BE TAKEN PRISONER IF AT ALL POSSIBLE. MAGISTER DENACHE'S ORDERS.
THAT RIGHT? MY ORDERS FROM COUNT DOOKU IS TO KILL 'EM.
LOOK, I DON'T CARE ONE WAY OR THE OTHER. I'M JUST PASSING ON THE ORDER. OBEY IT OR NOT. IT'S UP TO YOU.
SECURE THE JEDI UNTIL I CAN CONTACT THE COUNT AND DOUBLE-CHECK THIS.

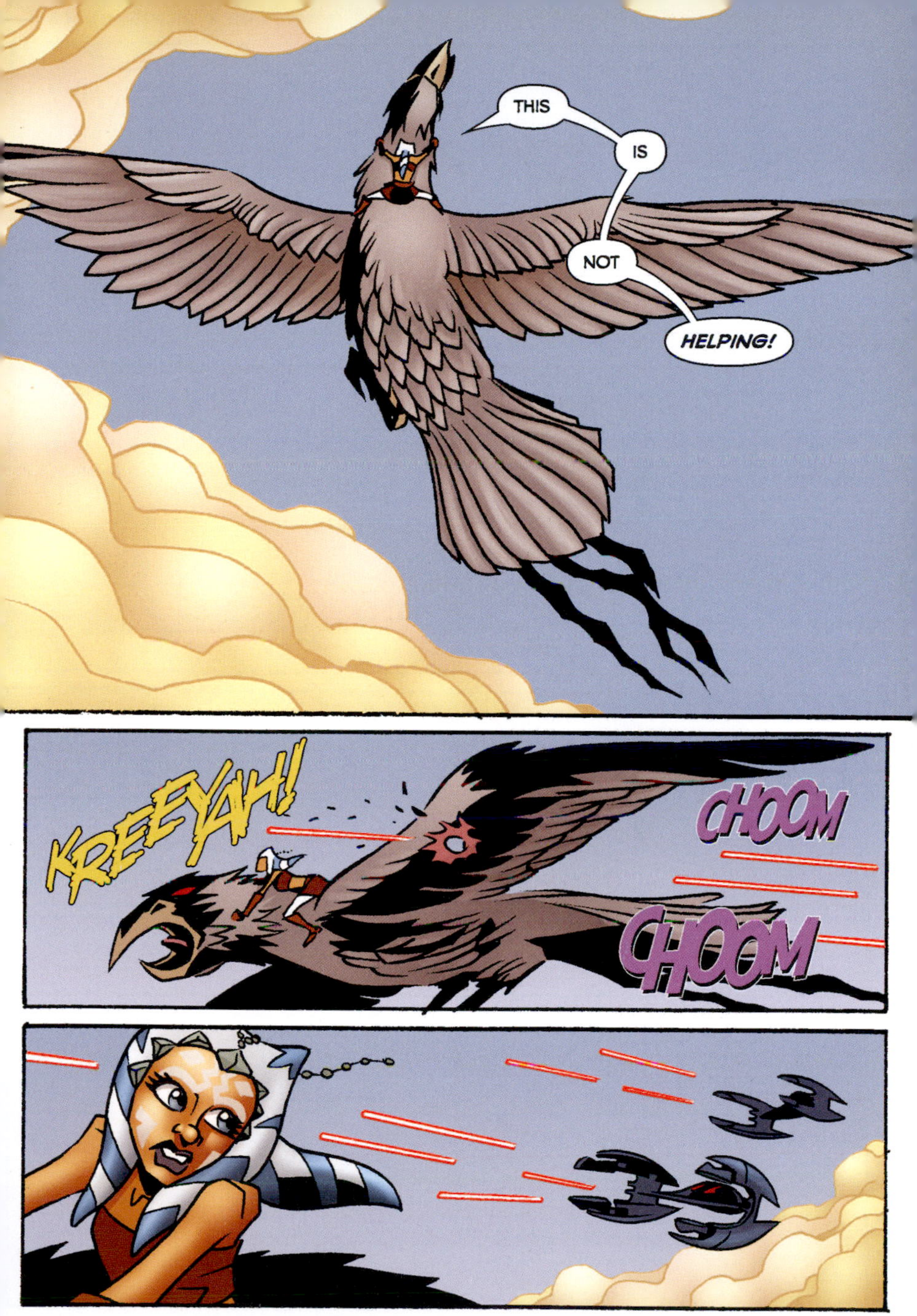
THIS
IS
NOT
HELPING!
KREEYAH!
CHOOM
CHOOM

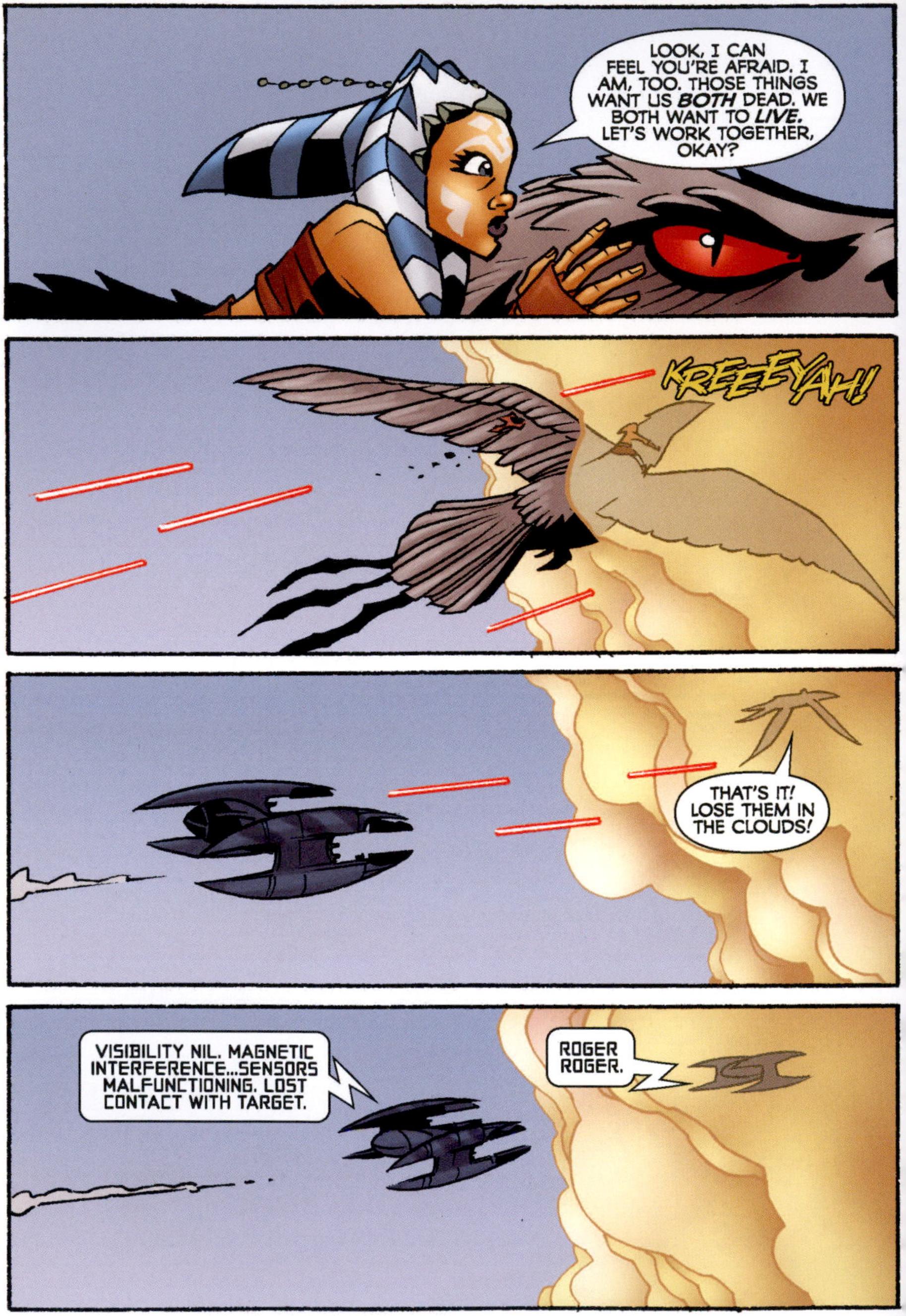
LOOK, I CAN FEEL YOU'RE AFRAID. I AM, TOO. THOSE THINGS WANT US BOTH DEAD. WE BOTH WANT TO LIVE. LET'S WORK TOGETHER, OKAY?
KREEEYAH!
THAT'S IT! LOSE THEM IN THE CLOUDS!
VISIBILITY NIL. MAGNETIC INTERFERENCE...SENSORS MALFUNCTIONING. LOST CONTACT WITH TARGET.
ROGER ROGER.

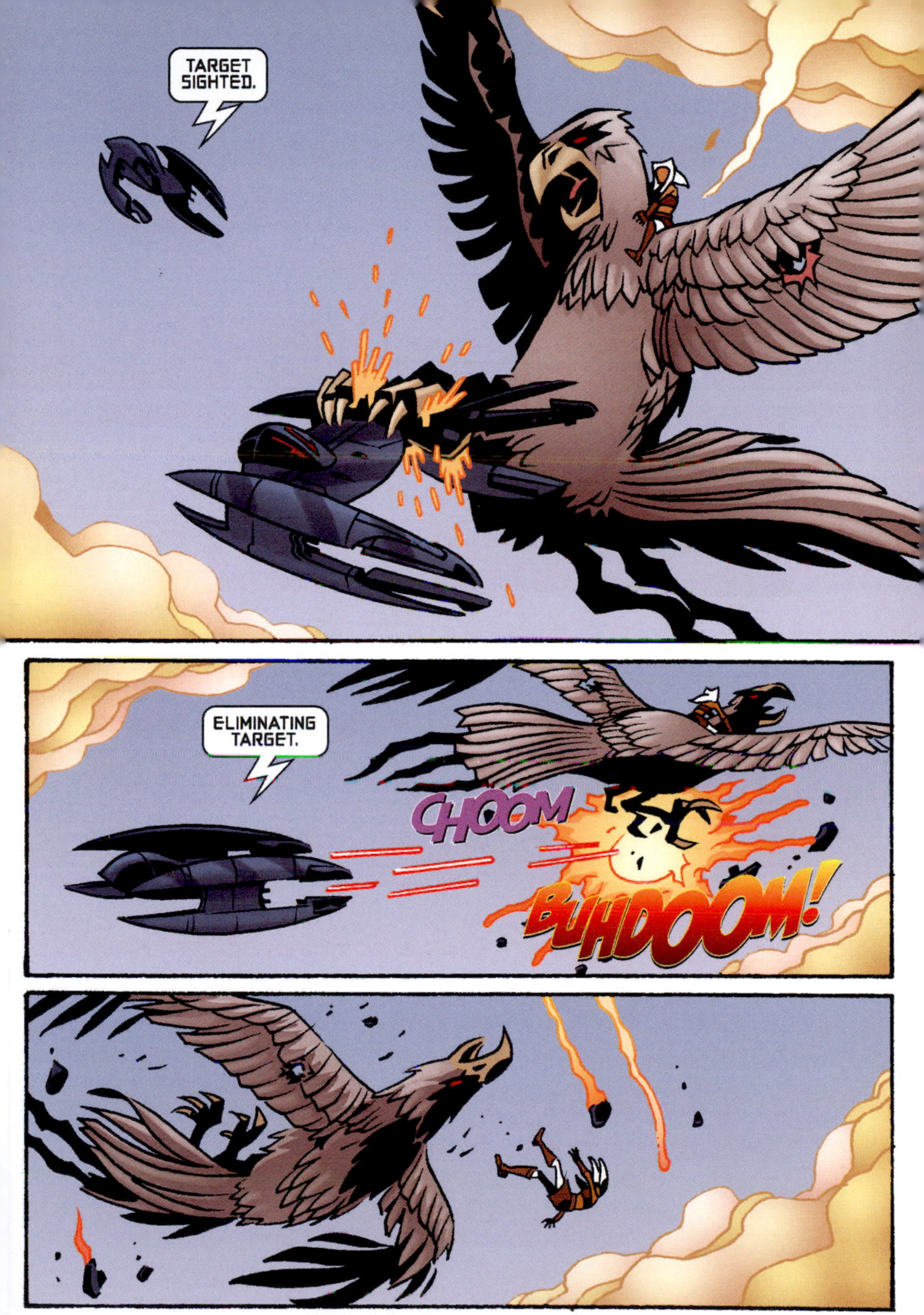
TARGET SIGHTED.
ELIMINATING TARGET.
CHOOM
BUHDOOM!

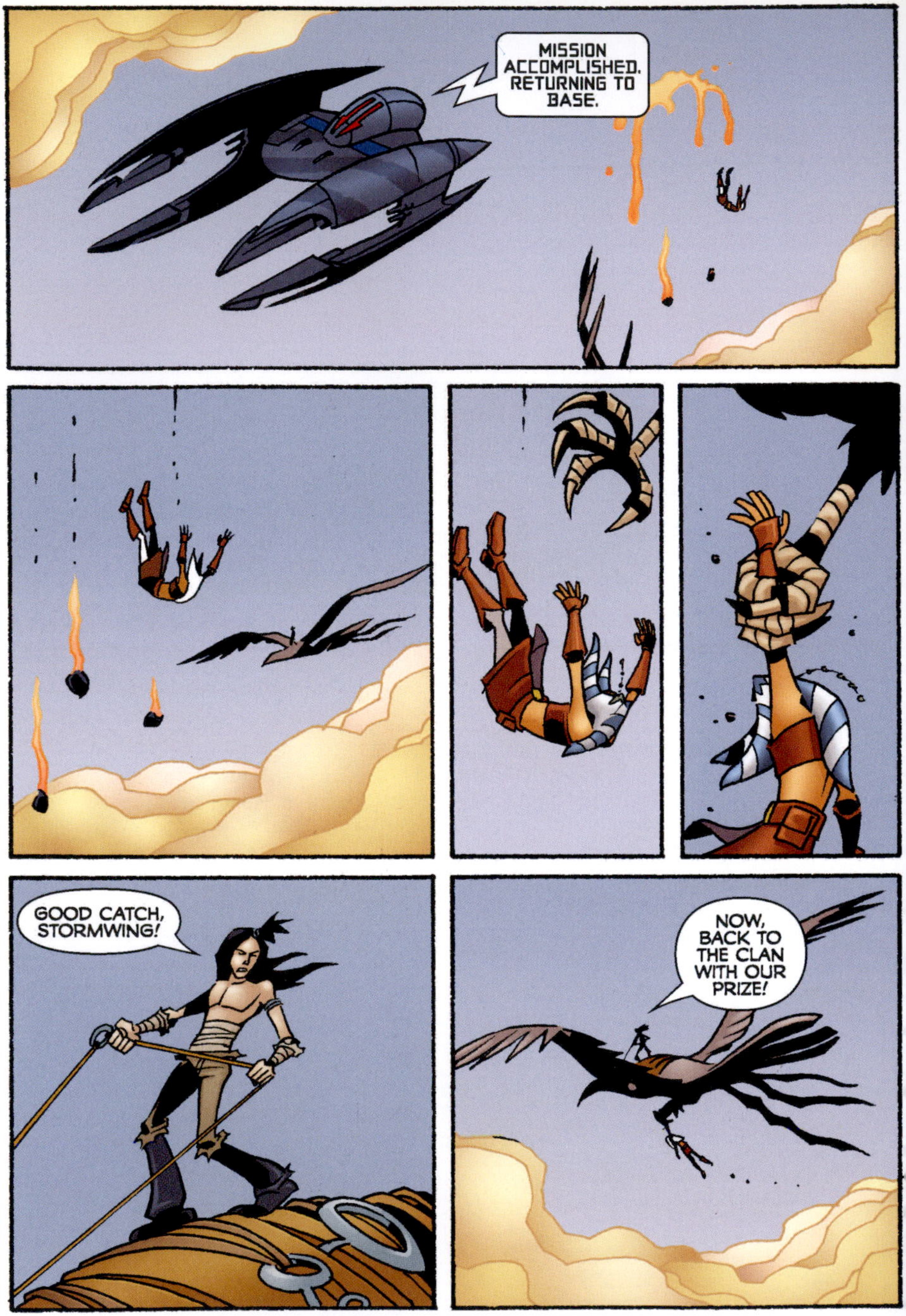
MISSION ACCOMPLISHED. RETURNING TO BASE.
GOOD CATCH, STORMWING!
NOW, BACK TO THE CLAN WITH OUR PRIZE!

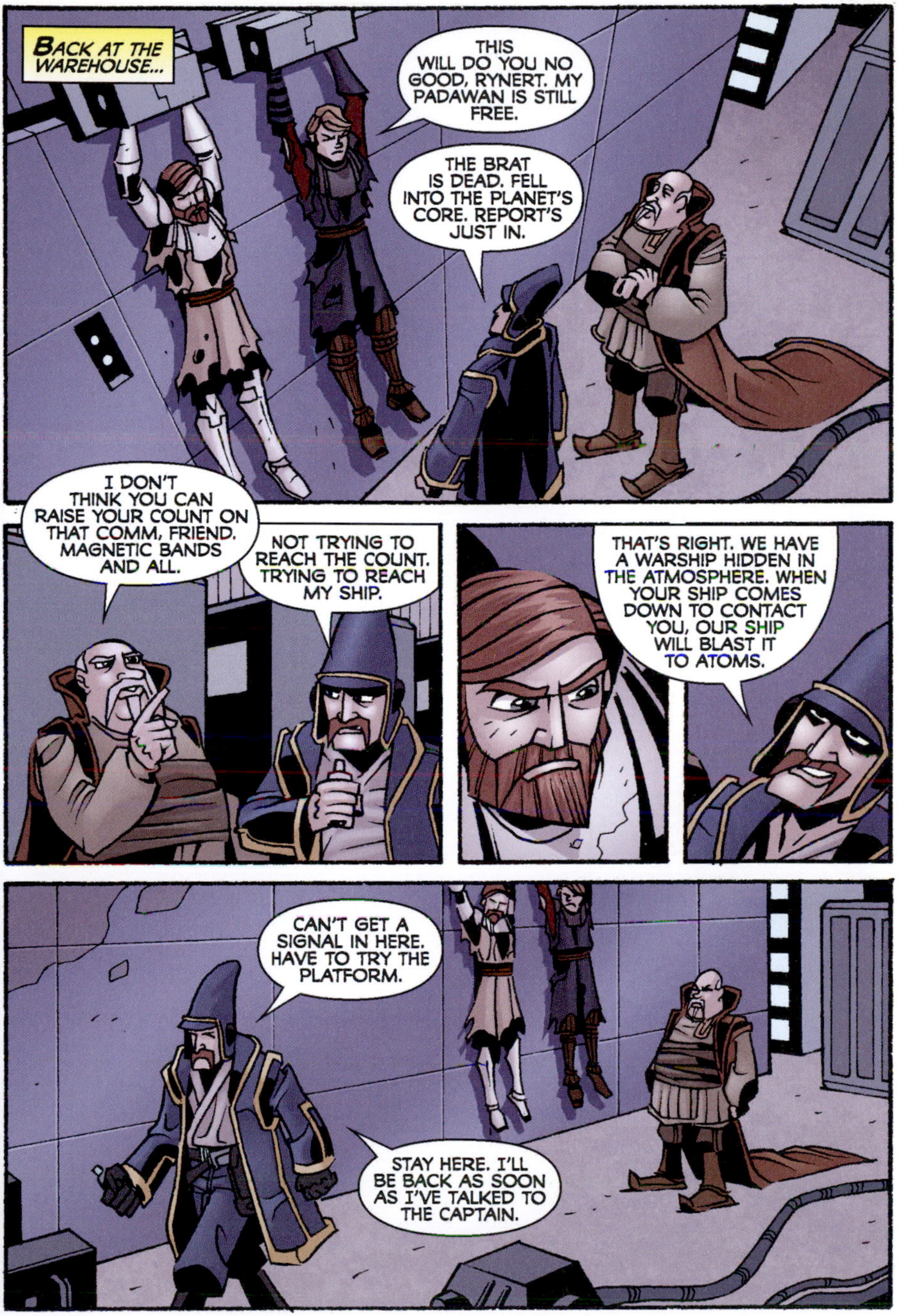
BACK AT THE WAREHOUSE...
THIS WILL DO YOU NO GOOD, RYNERT. MY PADAWAN IS STILL FREE.
THE BRAT IS DEAD. FELL INTO THE PLANET'S CORE. REPORT'S JUST IN.
I DON'T THINK YOU CAN RAISE YOUR COUNT ON THAT COMM, FRIEND. MAGNETIC BANDS AND ALL.
NOT TRYING TO REACH THE COUNT. TRYING TO REACH MY SHIP.
THAT'S RIGHT. WE HAVE A WARSHIP HIDDEN IN THE ATMOSPHERE. WHEN YOUR SHIP COMES DOWN TO CONTACT YOU, OUR SHIP WILL BLAST IT TO ATOMS.
CAN'T GET A SIGNAL IN HERE. HAVE TO TRY THE PLATFORM.
STAY HERE. I'LL BE BACK AS SOON AS I'VE TALKED TO THE CAPTAIN.

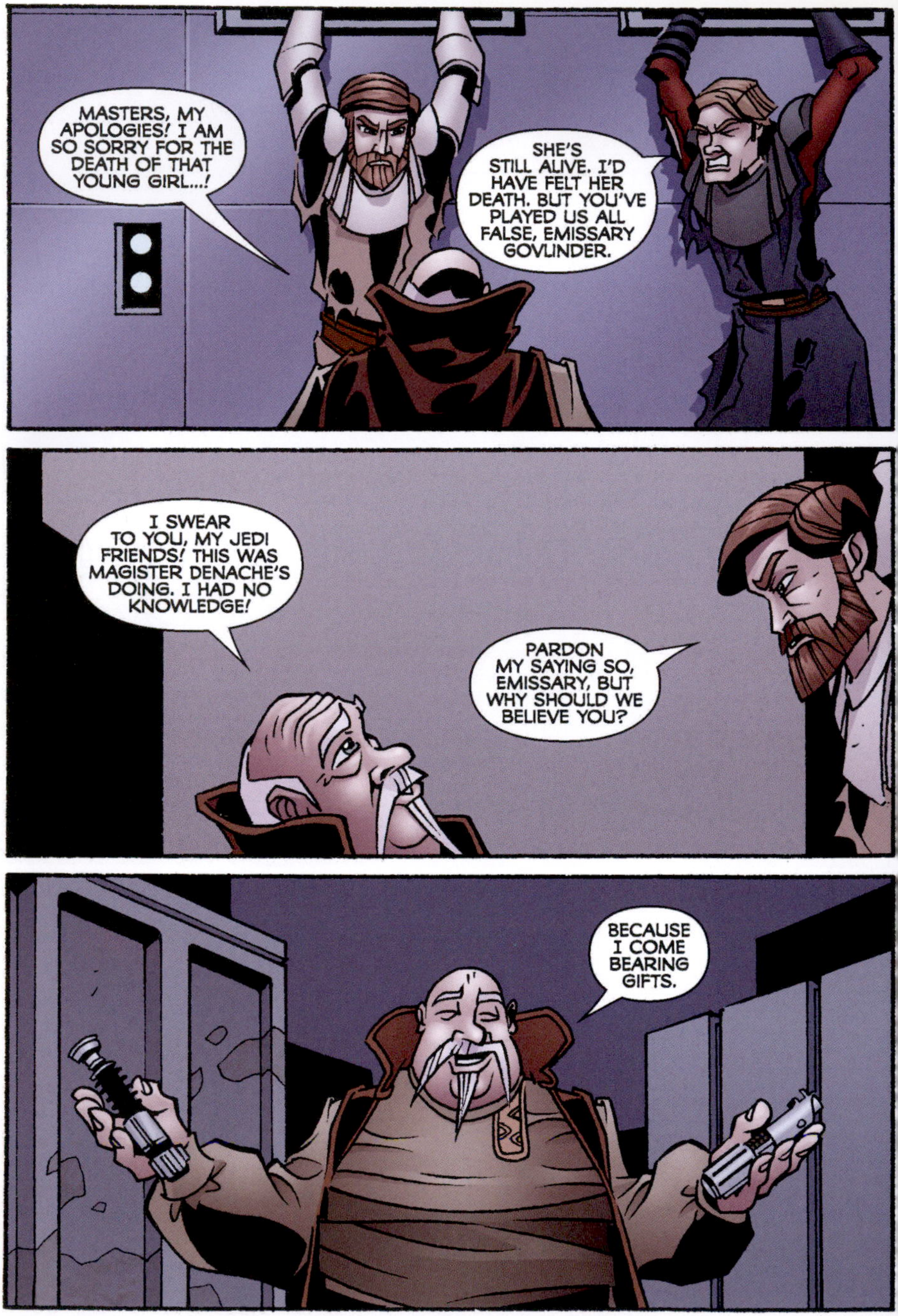
MASTERS, MY APOLOGIES! I AM SO SORRY FOR THE DEATH OF THAT YOUNG GIRL...!
SHE'S STILL ALIVE. I'D HAVE FELT HER DEATH. BUT YOU'VE PLAYED US ALL FALSE, EMISSARY GOVLINDER.
I SWEAR TO YOU, MY JEDI FRIENDS! THIS WAS MAGISTER DENACHE'S DOING. I HAD NO KNOWLEDGE!
PARDON MY SAYING SO, EMISSARY, BUT WHY SHOULD WE BELIEVE YOU?
BECAUSE I COME BEARING GIFTS.

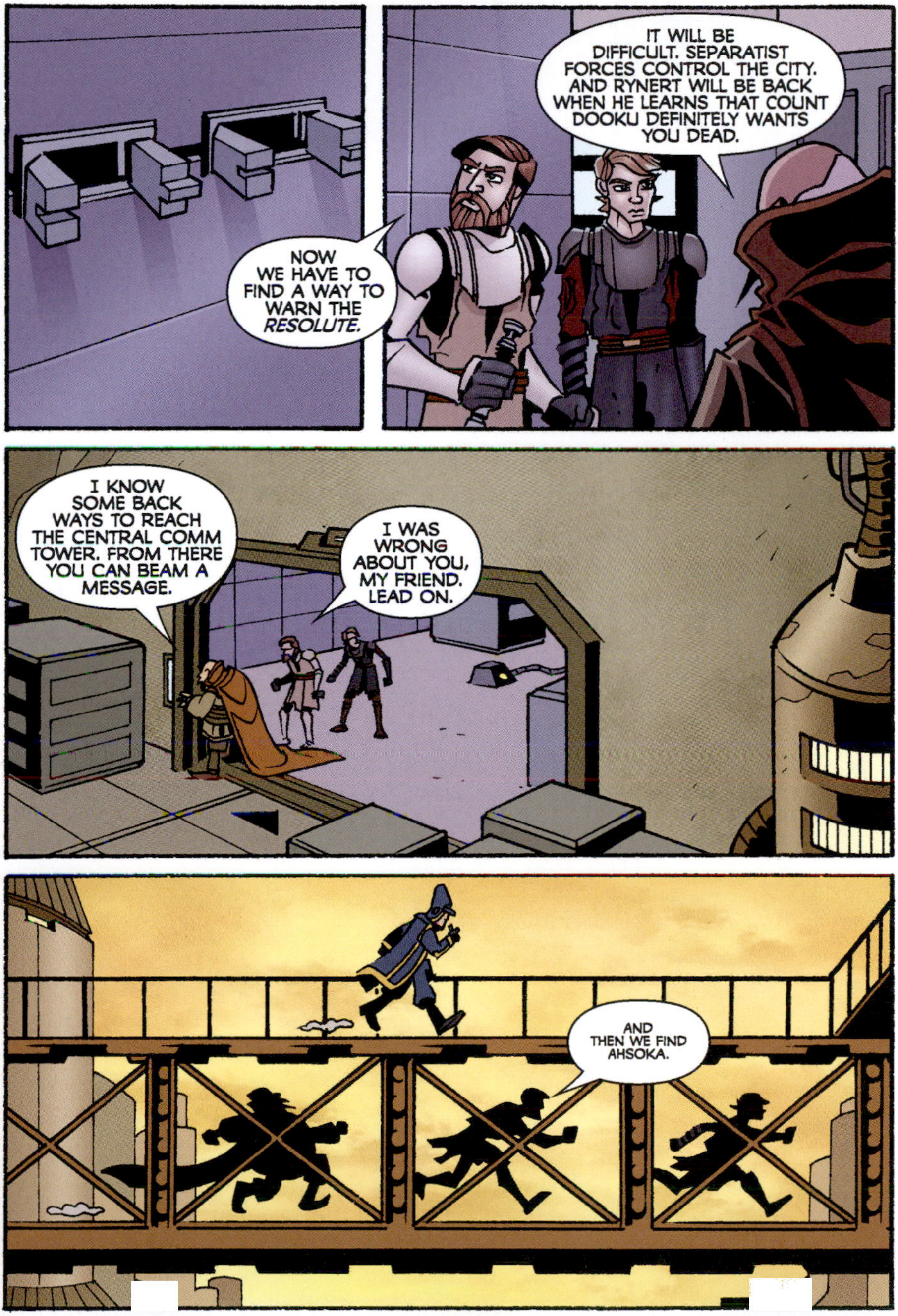
NOW WE HAVE TO FIND A WAY TO WARN THE *RESOLUTE.*
IT WILL BE DIFFICULT. SEPARATIST FORCES CONTROL THE CITY. AND RYNERT WILL BE BACK WHEN HE LEARNS THAT COUNT DOOKU DEFINITELY WANTS YOU DEAD.
I KNOW SOME BACK WAYS TO REACH THE CENTRAL COMM TOWER. FROM THERE YOU CAN BEAM A MESSAGE.
I WAS WRONG ABOUT YOU, MY FRIEND. LEAD ON.
AND THEN WE FIND AHSOKA.

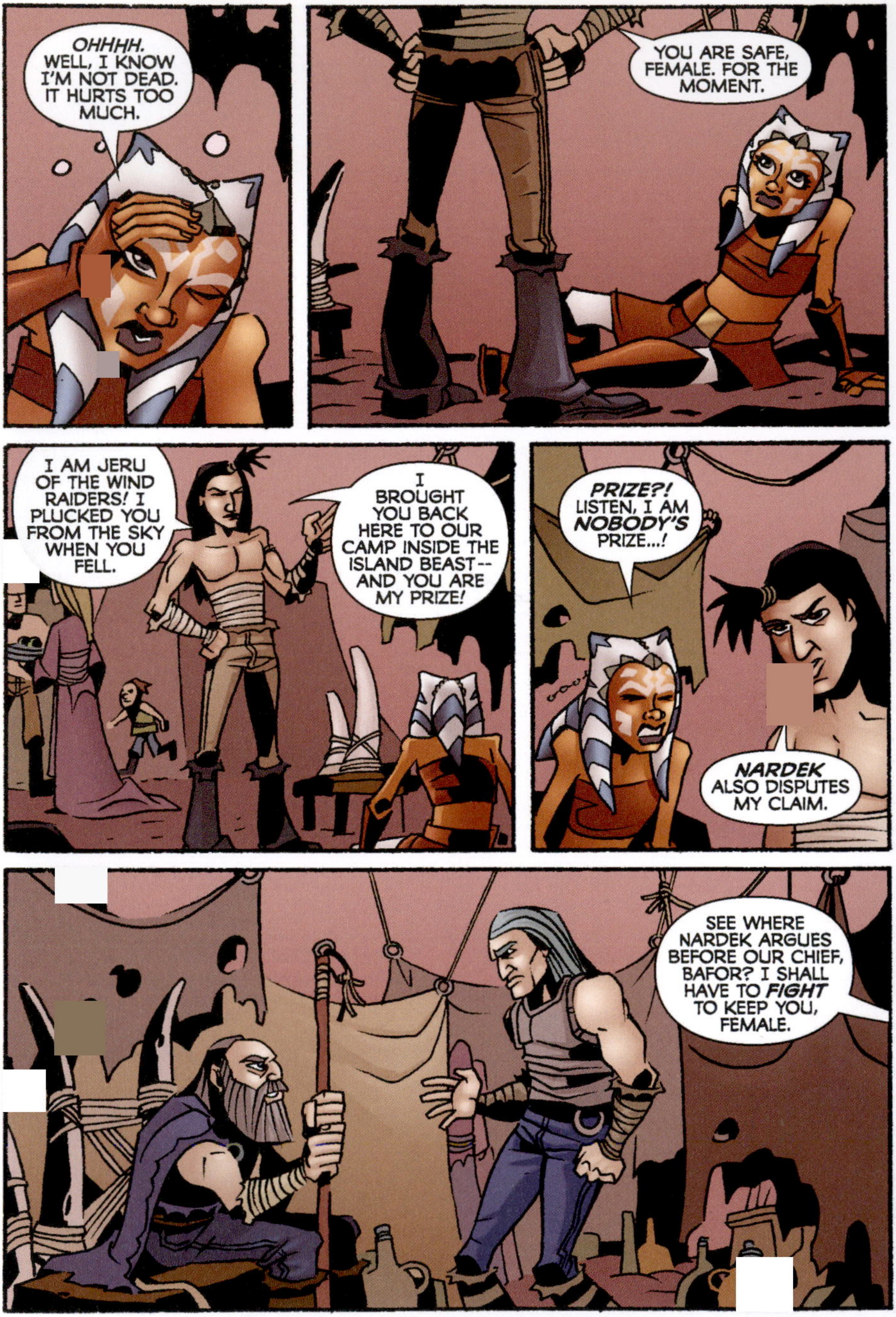
OHHHH. WELL, I KNOW I'M NOT DEAD. IT HURTS TOO MUCH.
YOU ARE SAFE, FEMALE. FOR THE MOMENT.
I AM JERU OF THE WIND RAIDERS! I PLUCKED YOU FROM THE SKY WHEN YOU FELL.
I BROUGHT YOU BACK HERE TO OUR CAMP INSIDE THE ISLAND BEAST-- AND YOU ARE MY PRIZE!
PRIZE?! LISTEN, I AM NOBODY'S PRIZE...!
NARDEK ALSO DISPUTES MY CLAIM.
SEE WHERE NARDEK ARGUES BEFORE OUR CHIEF, BAFOR? I SHALL HAVE TO FIGHT TO KEEP YOU, FEMALE.

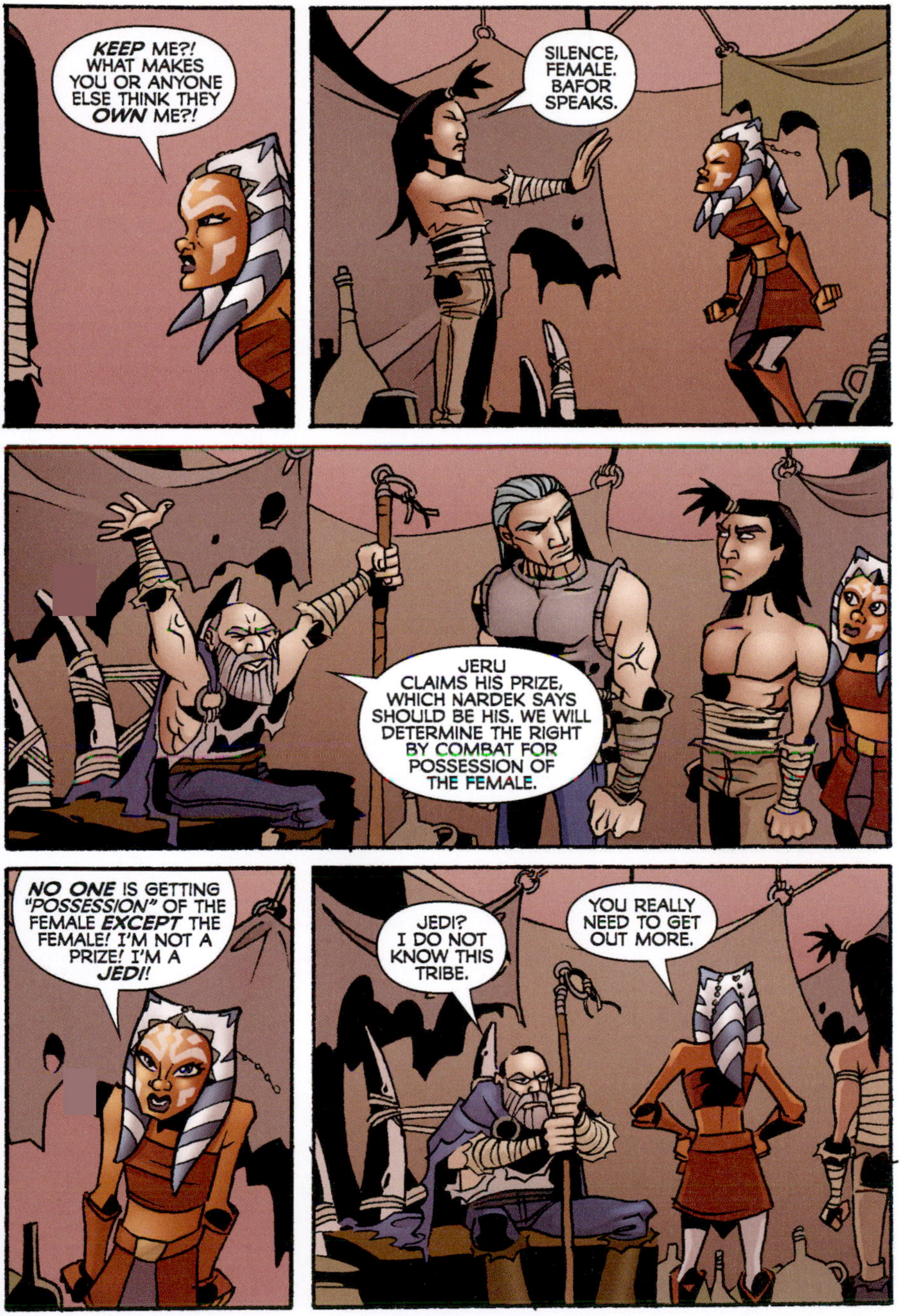
KEEP ME?! WHAT MAKES YOU OR ANYONE ELSE THINK THEY OWN ME?!
SILENCE, FEMALE. BAFOR SPEAKS.
JERU CLAIMS HIS PRIZE, WHICH NARDEK SAYS SHOULD BE HIS. WE WILL DETERMINE THE RIGHT BY COMBAT FOR POSSESSION OF THE FEMALE.
NO ONE IS GETTING "POSSESSION" OF THE FEMALE EXCEPT THE FEMALE! I'M NOT A PRIZE! I'M A JEDI!
JEDI? I DO NOT KNOW THIS TRIBE.
YOU REALLY NEED TO GET OUT MORE.

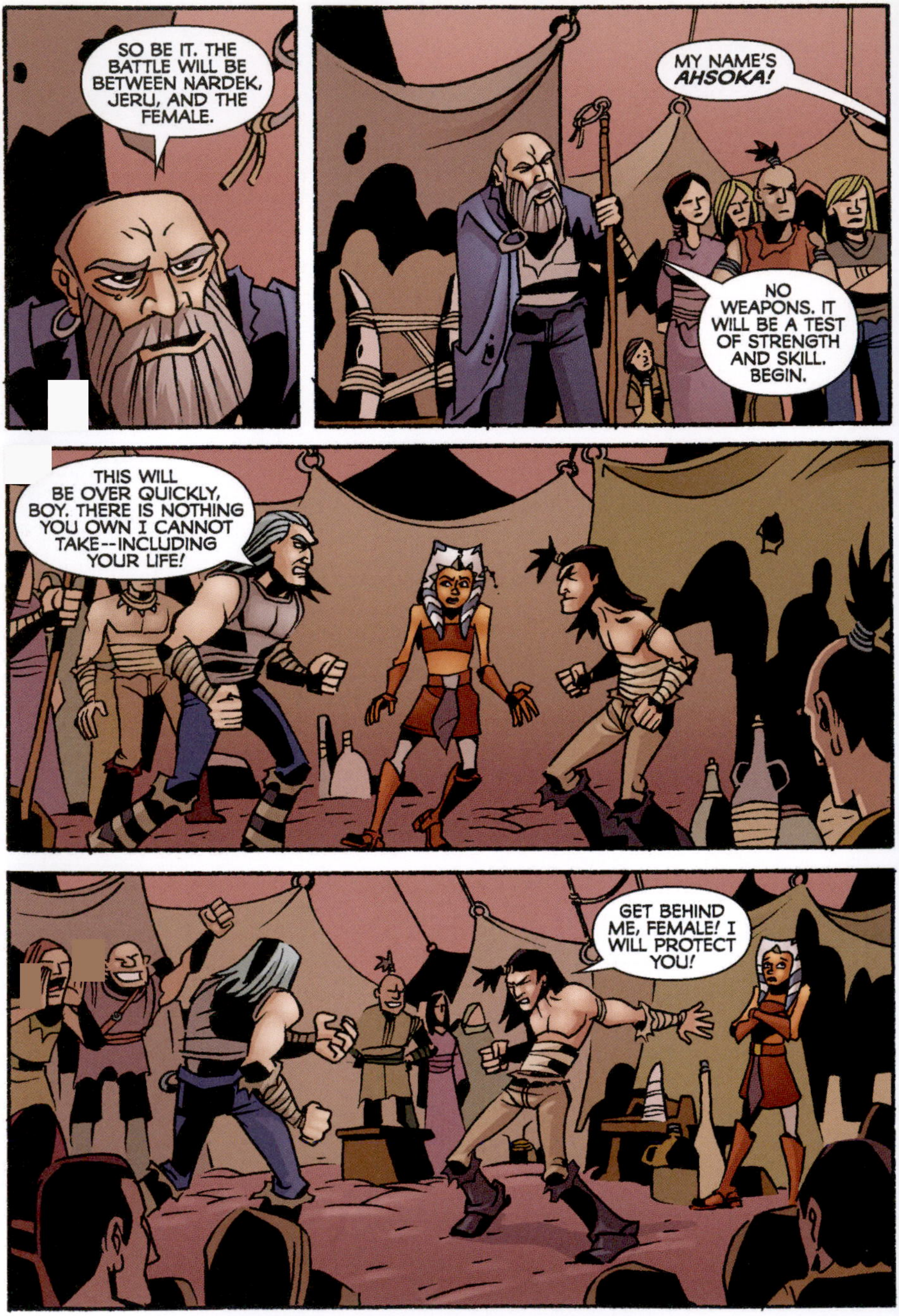
SO BE IT. THE BATTLE WILL BE BETWEEN NARDEK, JERU, AND THE FEMALE.
MY NAME'S *AHSOKA!*
NO WEAPONS. IT WILL BE A TEST OF STRENGTH AND SKILL. BEGIN.
THIS WILL BE OVER QUICKLY, BOY. THERE IS NOTHING YOU OWN I CANNOT TAKE--INCLUDING YOUR LIFE!
GET BEHIND ME, FEMALE! I WILL PROTECT YOU!

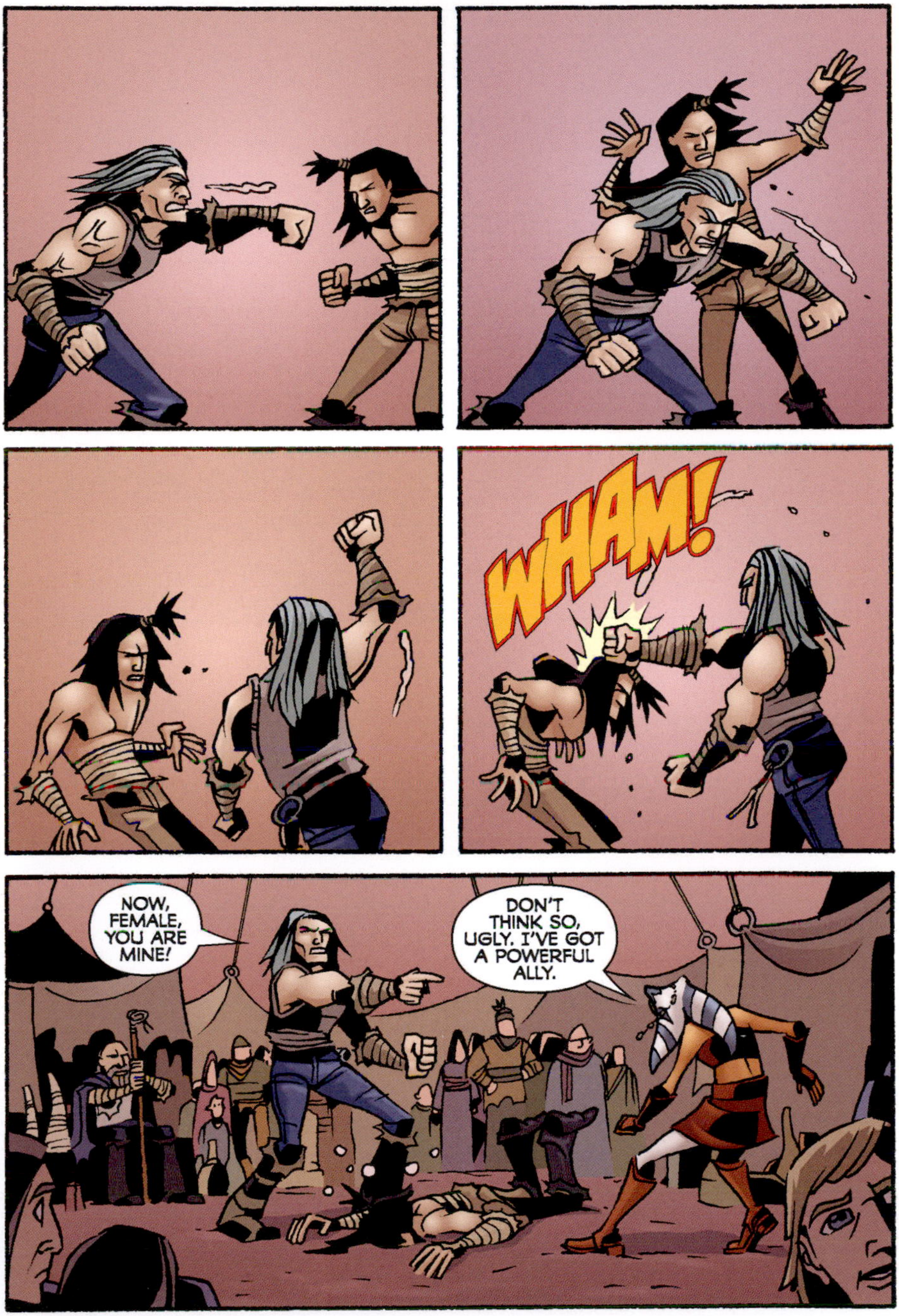
WHAM!
NOW, FEMALE, YOU ARE MINE!
DON'T THINK SO, UGLY. I'VE GOT A POWERFUL ALLY.

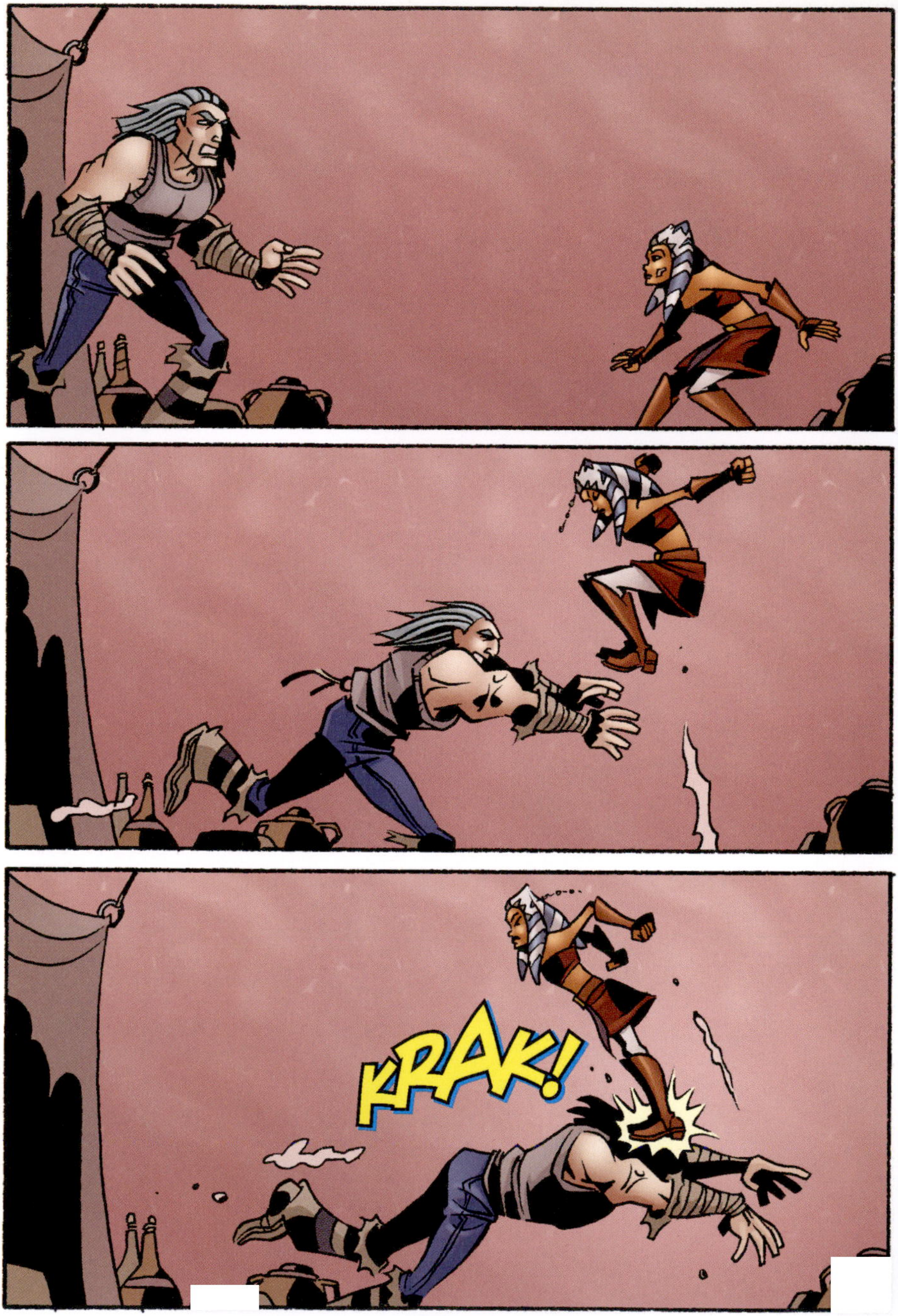
KRAK!

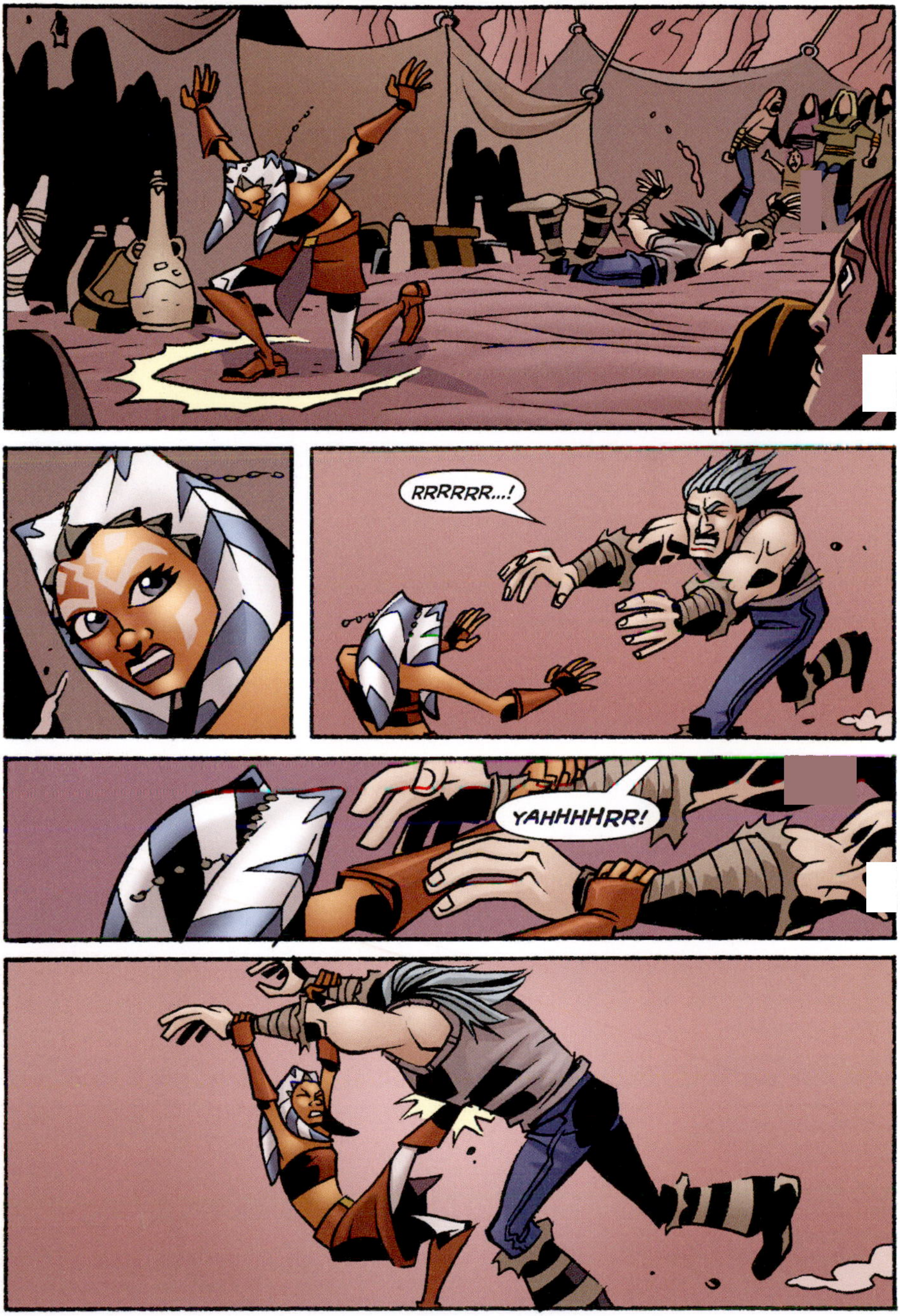
RRRRRR...!
YAHHHHRR!

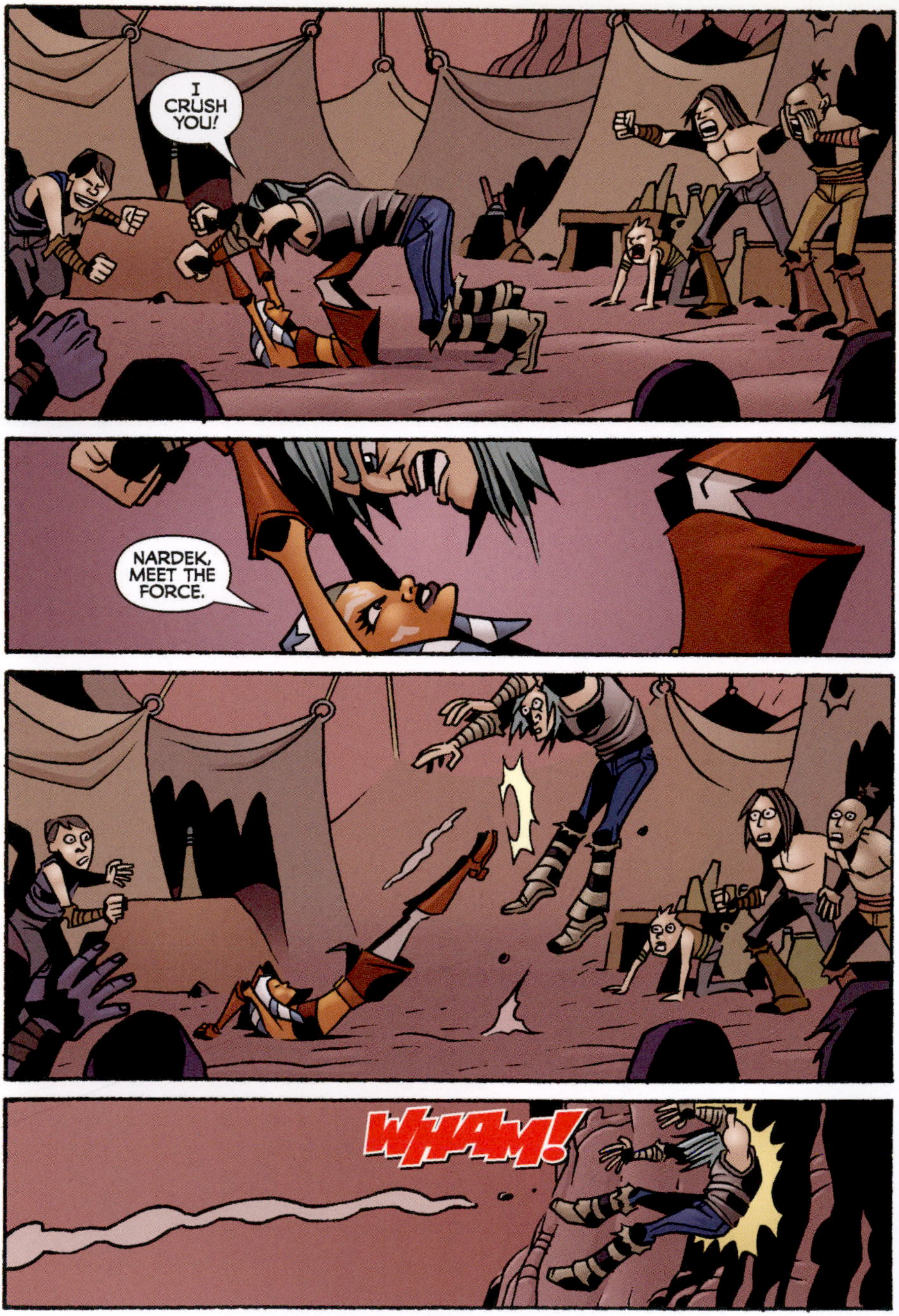
I CRUSH YOU!
NARDEK, MEET THE FORCE.
WHAM!

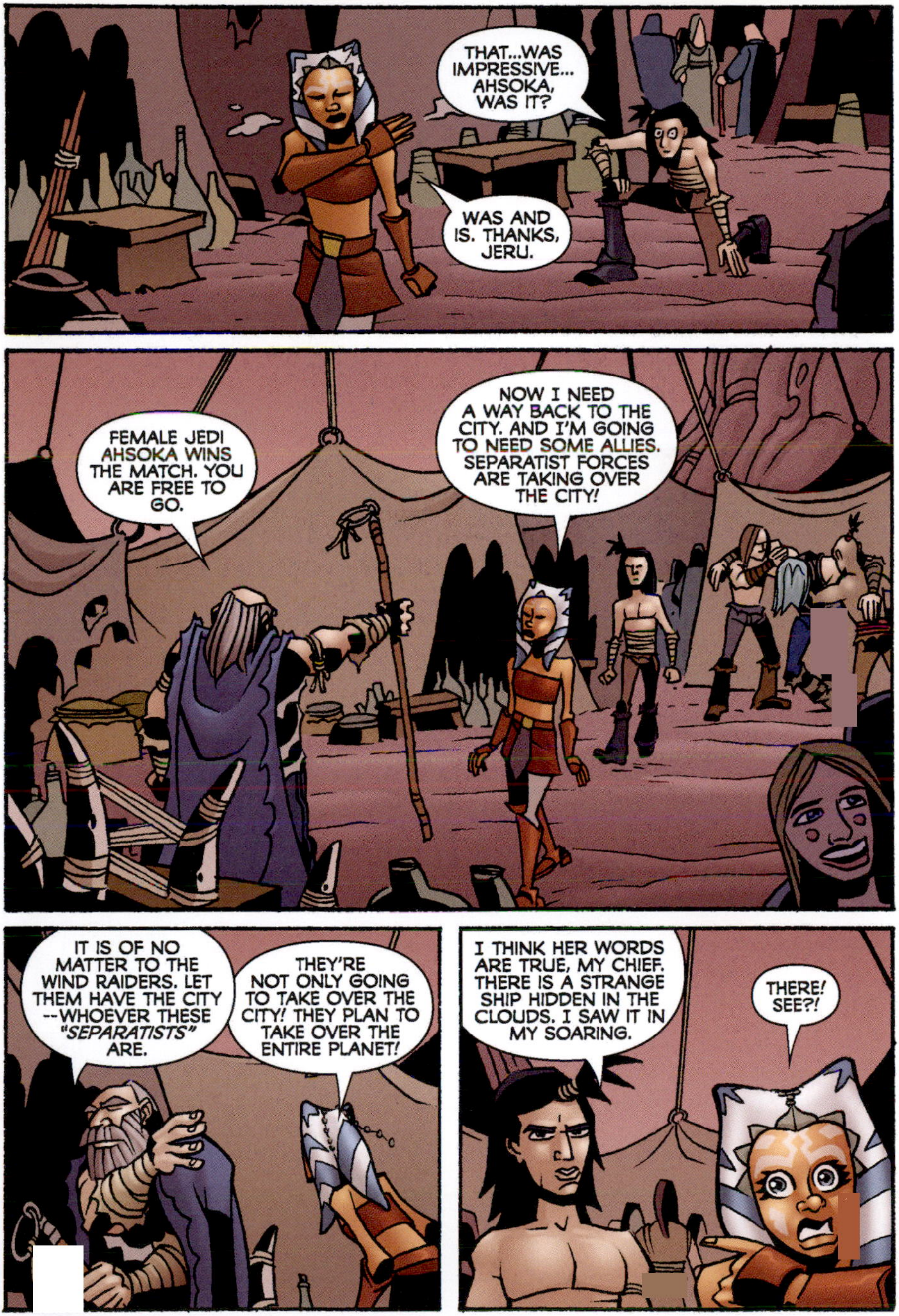
THAT...WAS IMPRESSIVE... AHSOKA, WAS IT?
WAS AND IS. THANKS, JERU.
FEMALE JEDI AHSOKA WINS THE MATCH. YOU ARE FREE TO GO.
NOW I NEED A WAY BACK TO THE CITY. AND I'M GOING TO NEED SOME ALLIES. SEPARATIST FORCES ARE TAKING OVER THE CITY!
IT IS OF NO MATTER TO THE WIND RAIDERS. LET THEM HAVE THE CITY --WHOEVER THESE "SEPARATISTS" ARE.
THEY'RE NOT ONLY GOING TO TAKE OVER THE CITY! THEY PLAN TO TAKE OVER THE ENTIRE PLANET!
I THINK HER WORDS ARE TRUE, MY CHIEF. THERE IS A STRANGE SHIP HIDDEN IN THE CLOUDS. I SAW IT IN MY SOARING.
THERE! SEE?!

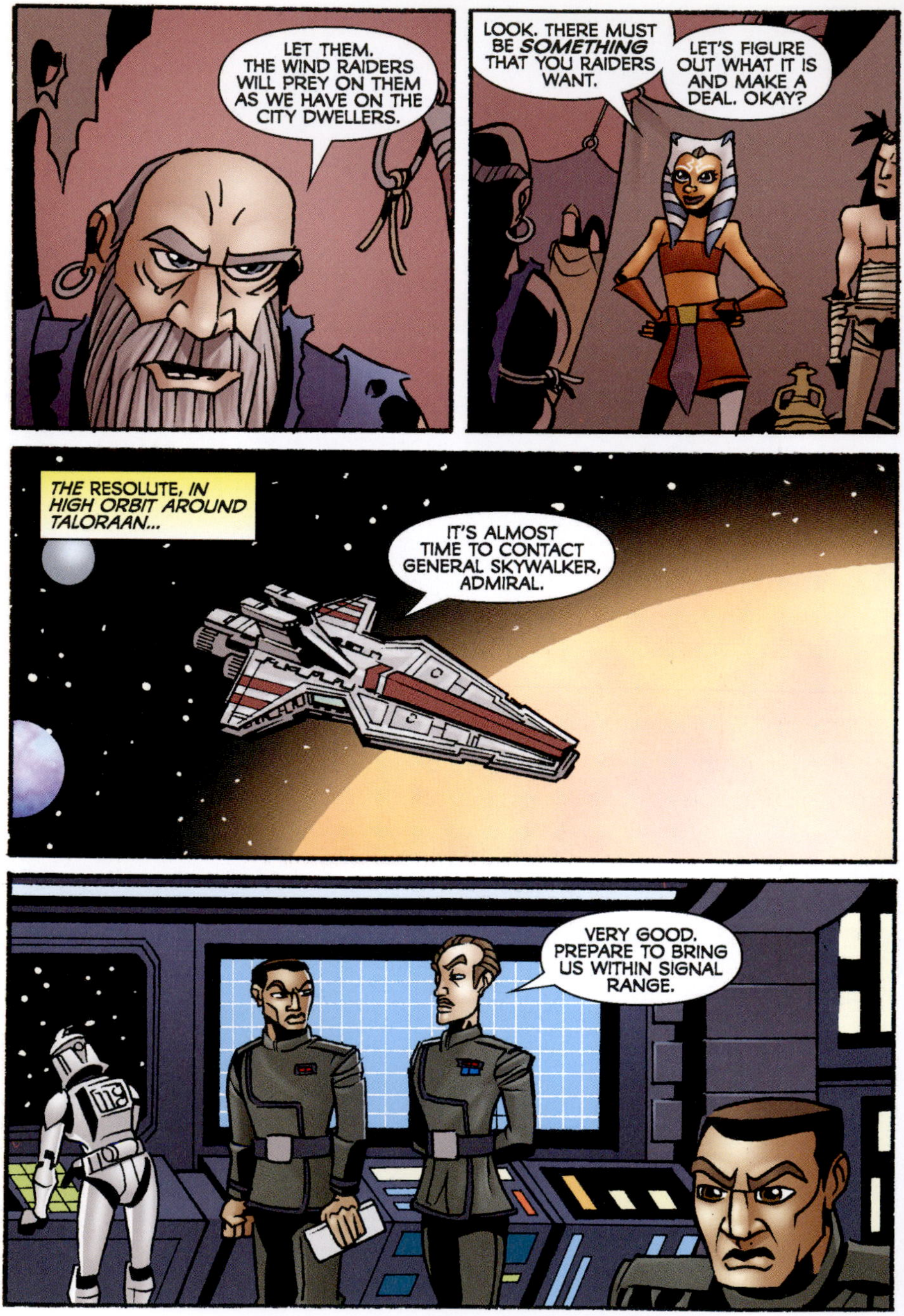
LET THEM. THE WIND RAIDERS WILL PREY ON THEM AS WE HAVE ON THE CITY DWELLERS.
LOOK. THERE MUST BE *SOMETHING* THAT YOU RAIDERS WANT.
LET'S FIGURE OUT WHAT IT IS AND MAKE A DEAL. OKAY?
THE RESOLUTE, *IN HIGH ORBIT AROUND TALORAAN...*
IT'S ALMOST TIME TO CONTACT GENERAL SKYWALKER, ADMIRAL.
VERY GOOD. PREPARE TO BRING US WITHIN SIGNAL RANGE.

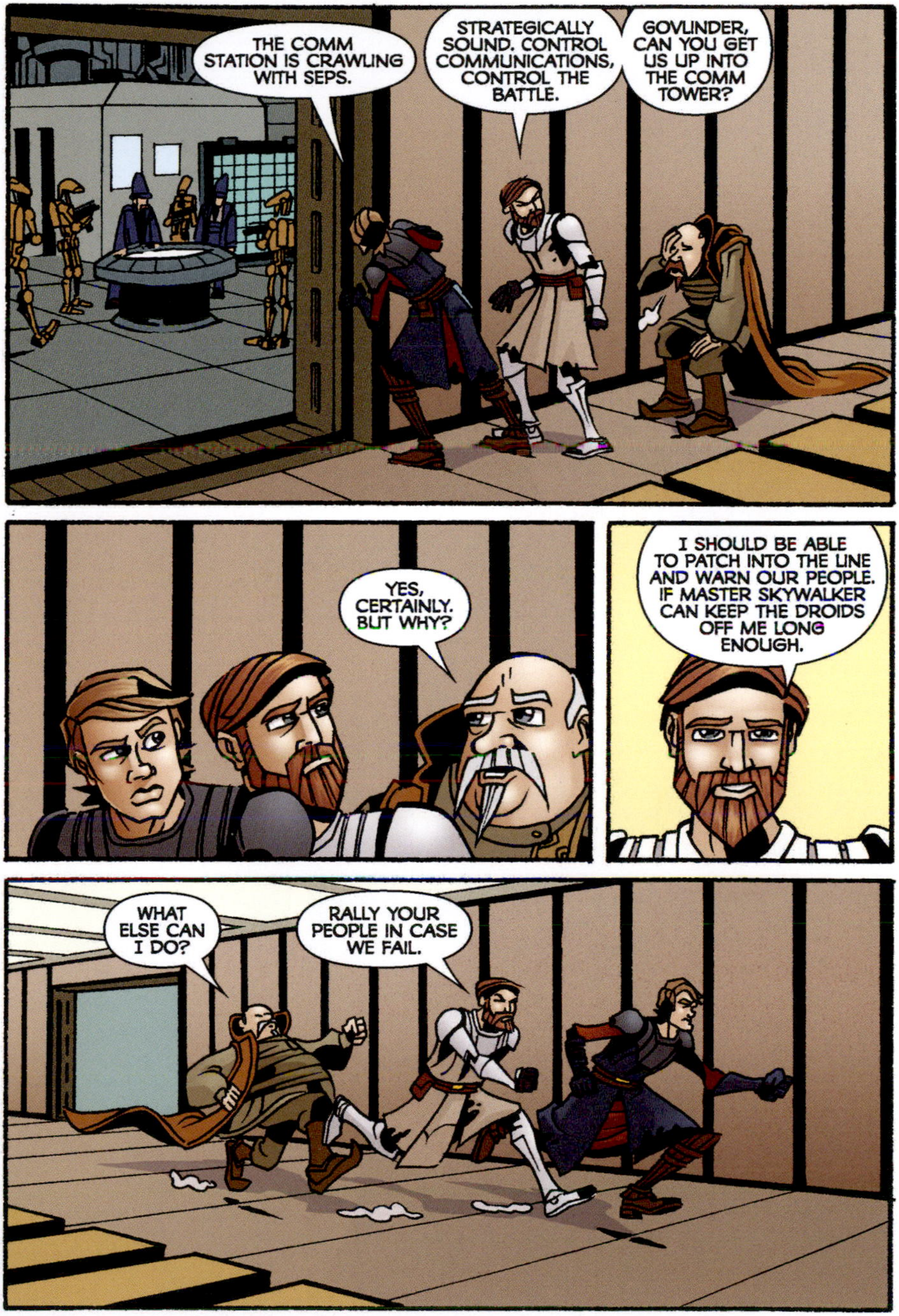
THE COMM STATION IS CRAWLING WITH SEPS.
STRATEGICALLY SOUND. CONTROL COMMUNICATIONS, CONTROL THE BATTLE.
GOVLINDER, CAN YOU GET US UP INTO THE COMM TOWER?
YES, CERTAINLY. BUT WHY?
I SHOULD BE ABLE TO PATCH INTO THE LINE AND WARN OUR PEOPLE. IF MASTER SKYWALKER CAN KEEP THE DROIDS OFF ME LONG ENOUGH.
WHAT ELSE CAN I DO?
RALLY YOUR PEOPLE IN CASE WE FAIL.

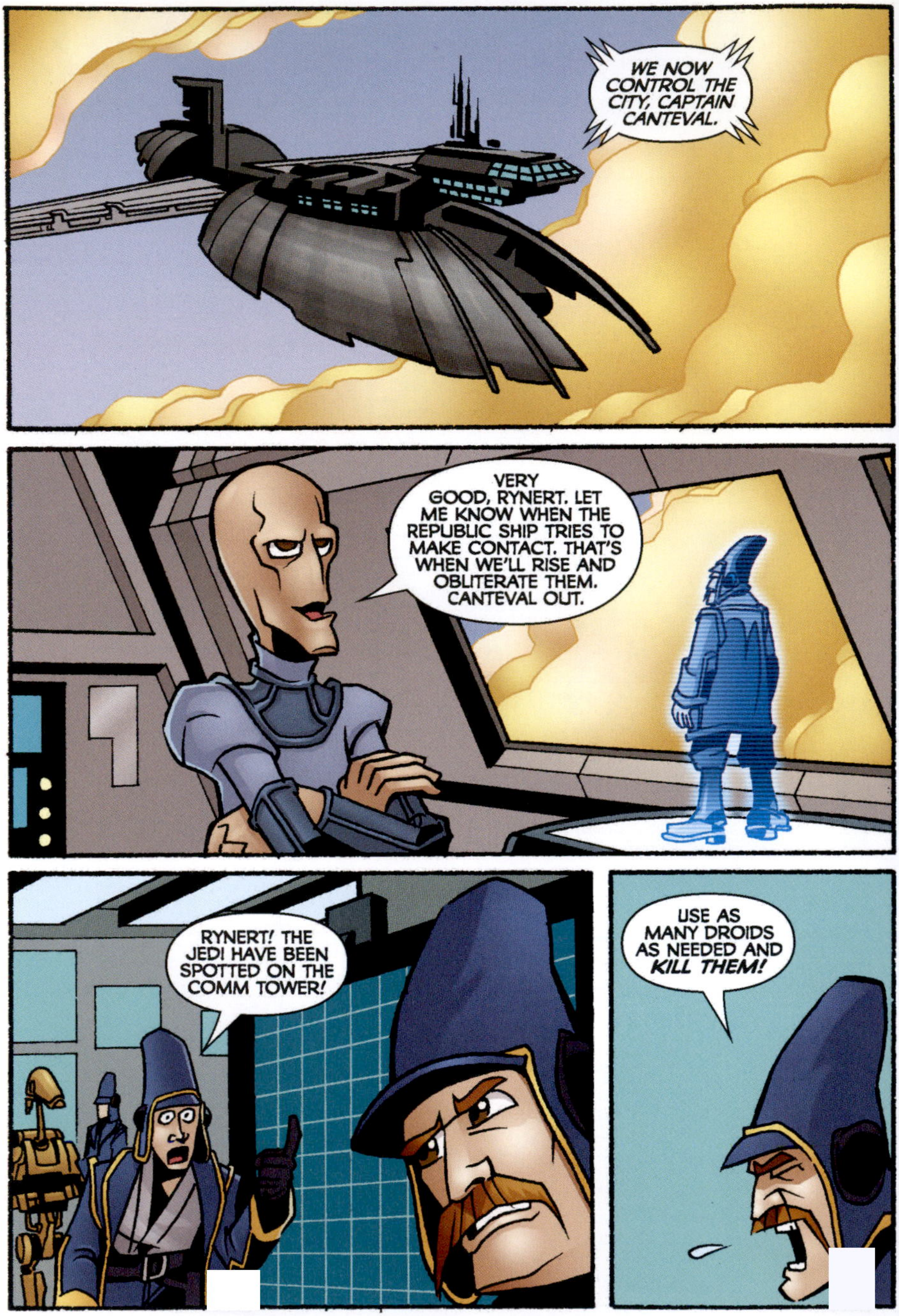
WE NOW CONTROL THE CITY, CAPTAIN CANTEVAL.
VERY GOOD, RYNERT. LET ME KNOW WHEN THE REPUBLIC SHIP TRIES TO MAKE CONTACT. THAT'S WHEN WE'LL RISE AND OBLITERATE THEM. CANTEVAL OUT.
RYNERT! THE JEDI HAVE BEEN SPOTTED ON THE COMM TOWER!
USE AS MANY DROIDS AS NEEDED AND KILL THEM!

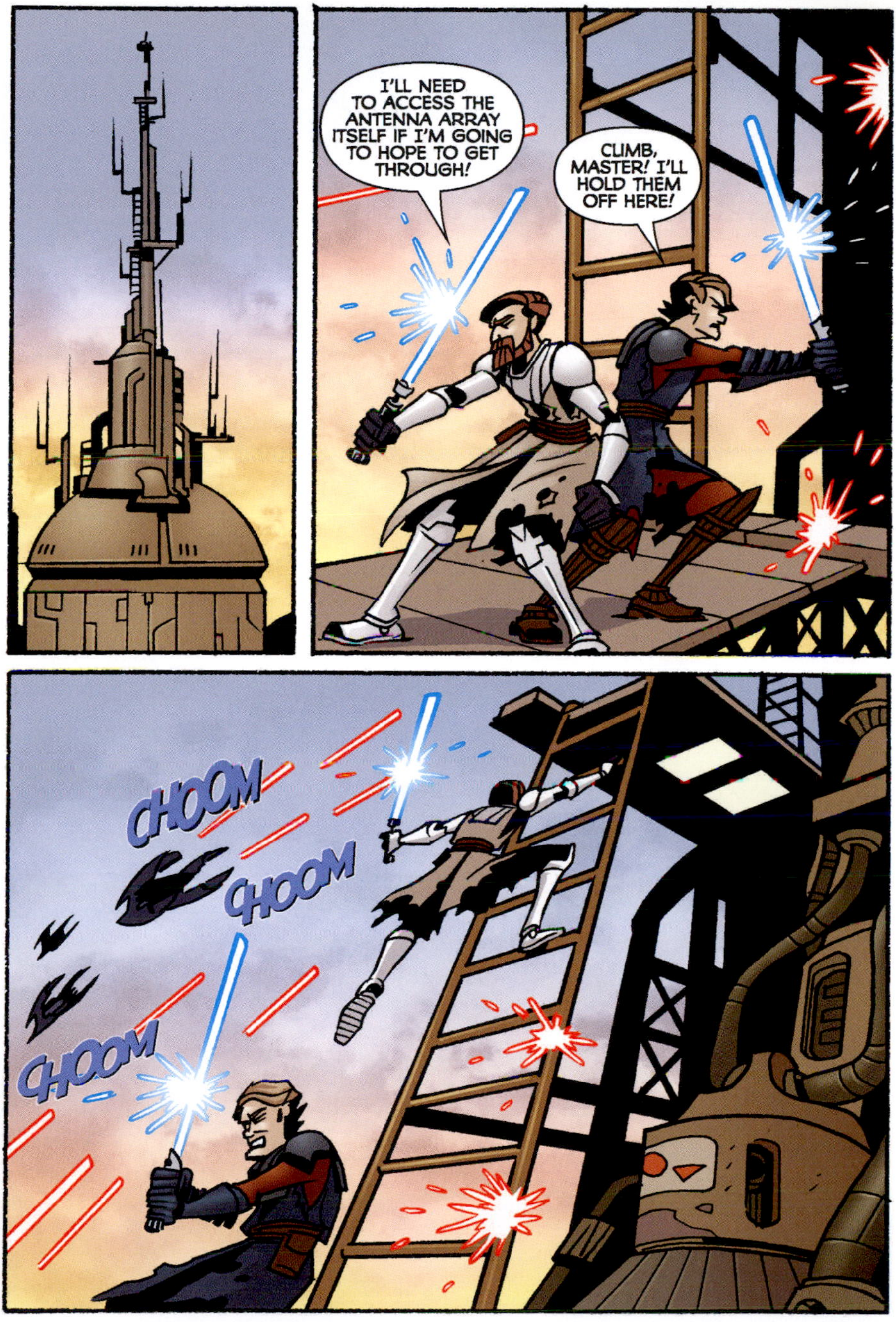
I'LL NEED TO ACCESS THE ANTENNA ARRAY ITSELF IF I'M GOING TO HOPE TO GET THROUGH!
CLIMB, MASTER! I'LL HOLD THEM OFF HERE!
CHOOM
CHOOM
CHOOM

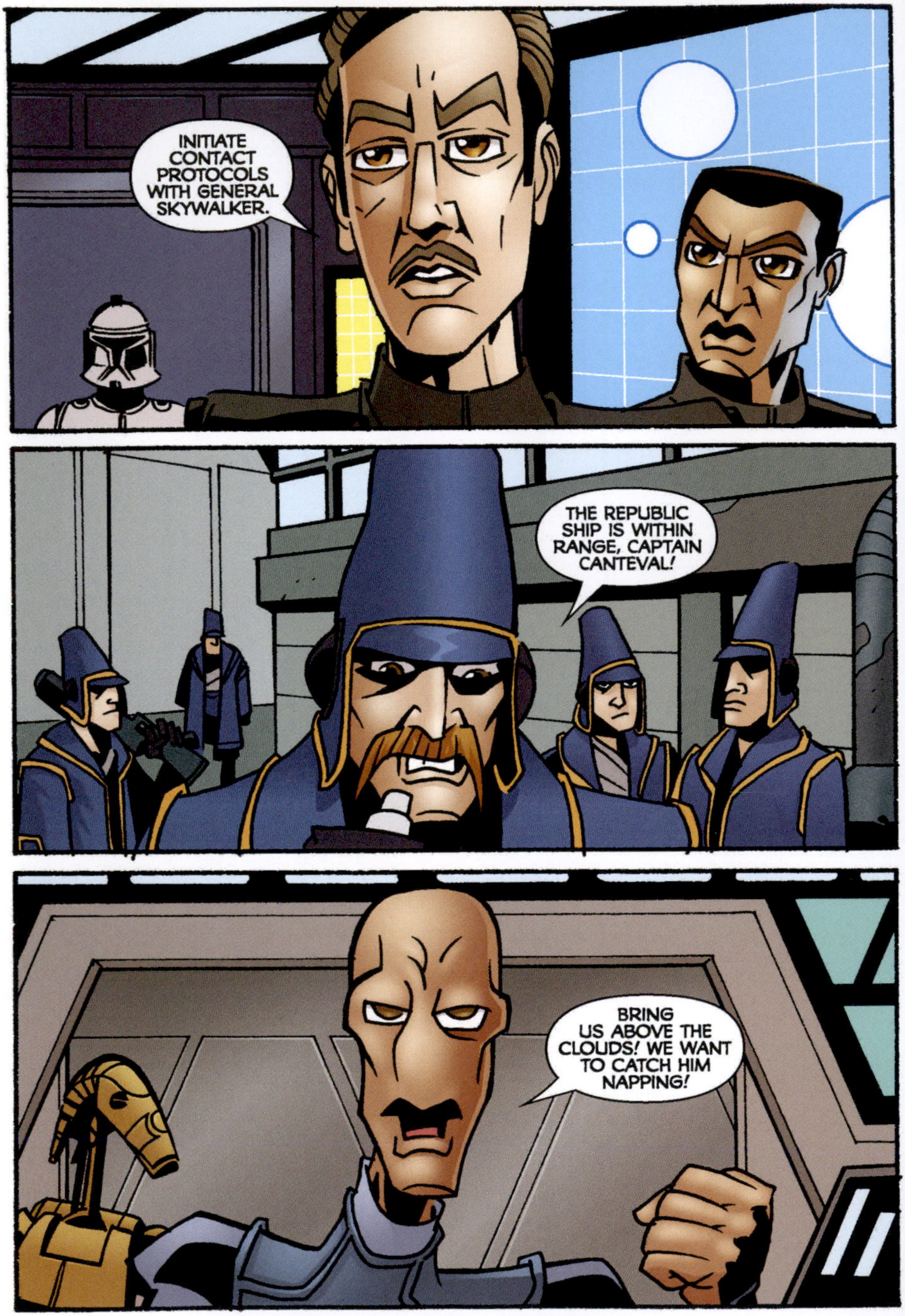
INITIATE CONTACT PROTOCOLS WITH GENERAL SKYWALKER.
THE REPUBLIC SHIP IS WITHIN RANGE, CAPTAIN CANTEVAL!
BRING US ABOVE THE CLOUDS! WE WANT TO CATCH HIM NAPPING!

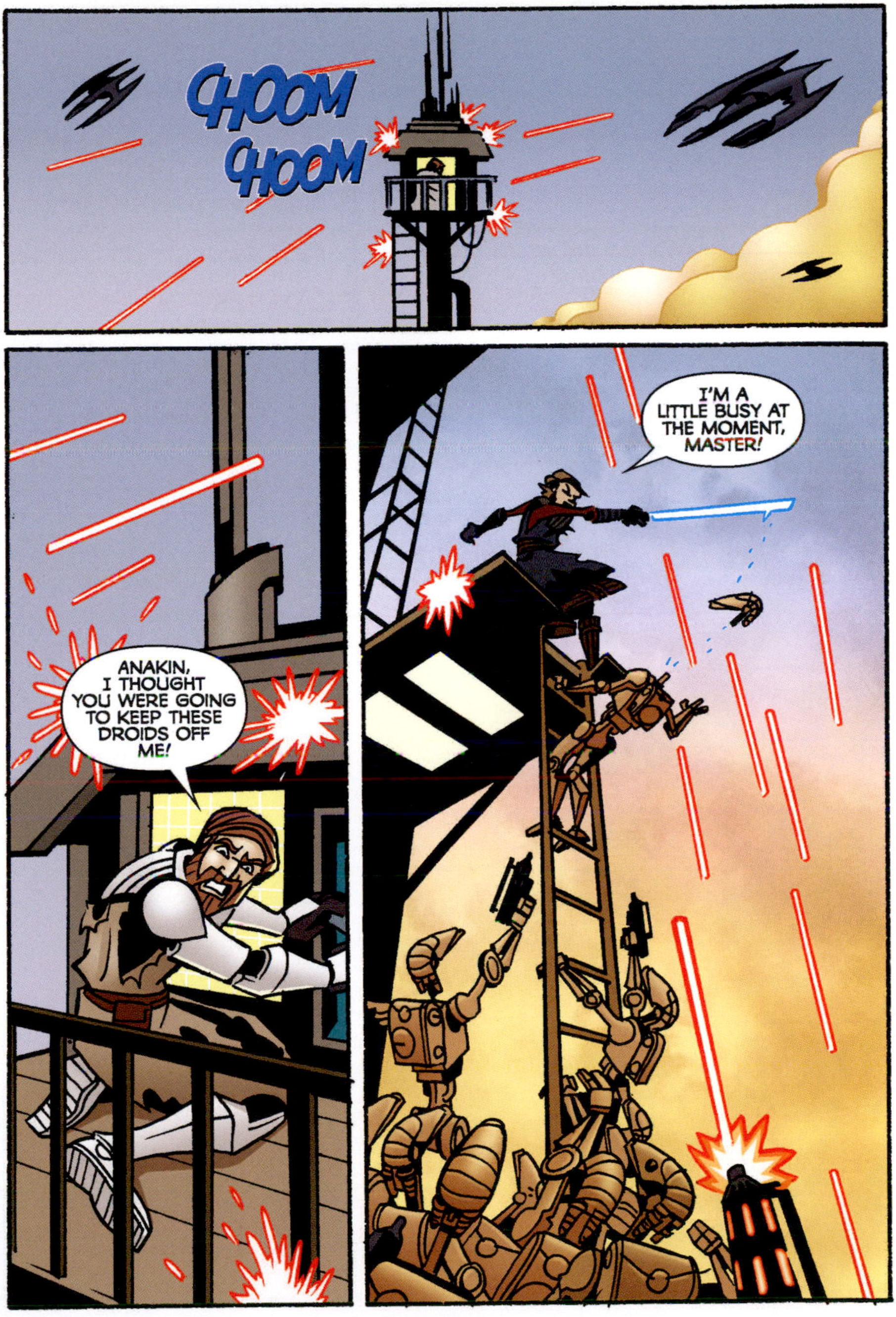
CHOOM
CHOOM
ANAKIN, I THOUGHT YOU WERE GOING TO KEEP THESE DROIDS OFF ME!
I'M A LITTLE BUSY AT THE MOMENT, MASTER!

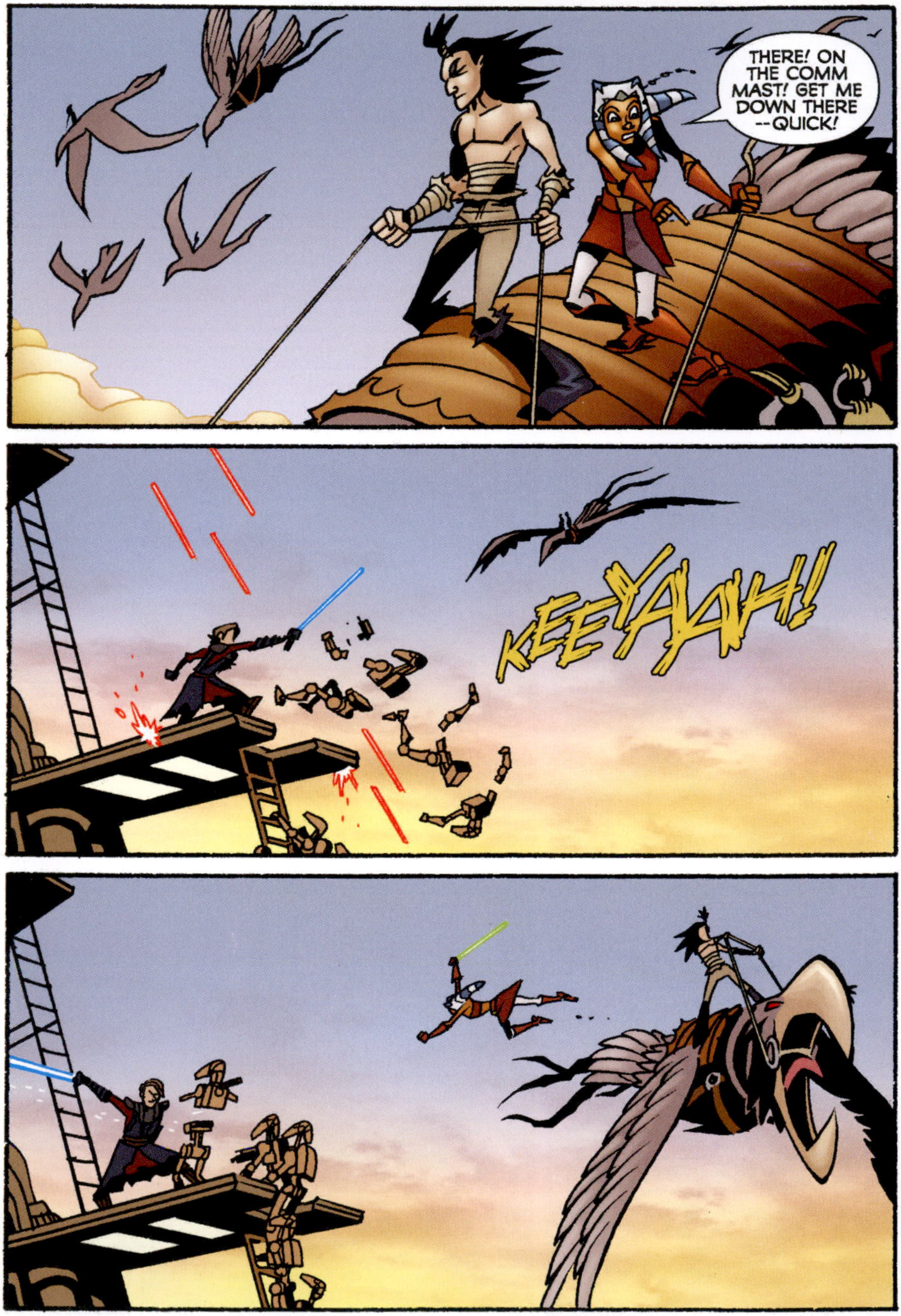
THERE! ON THE COMM MAST! GET ME DOWN THERE --QUICK!
KEEYAAH!

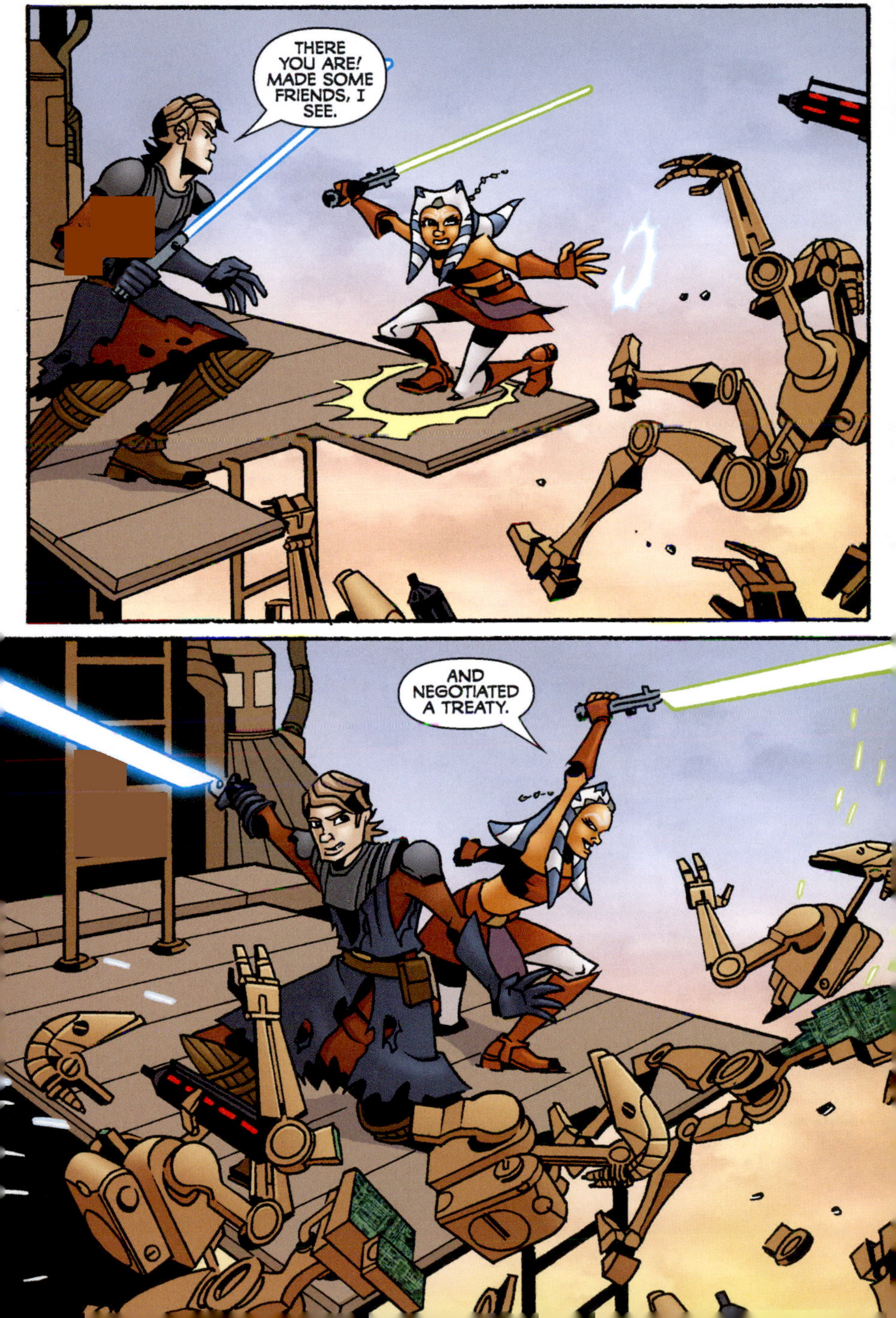
THERE YOU ARE! MADE SOME FRIENDS, I SEE.
AND NEGOTIATED A TREATY.

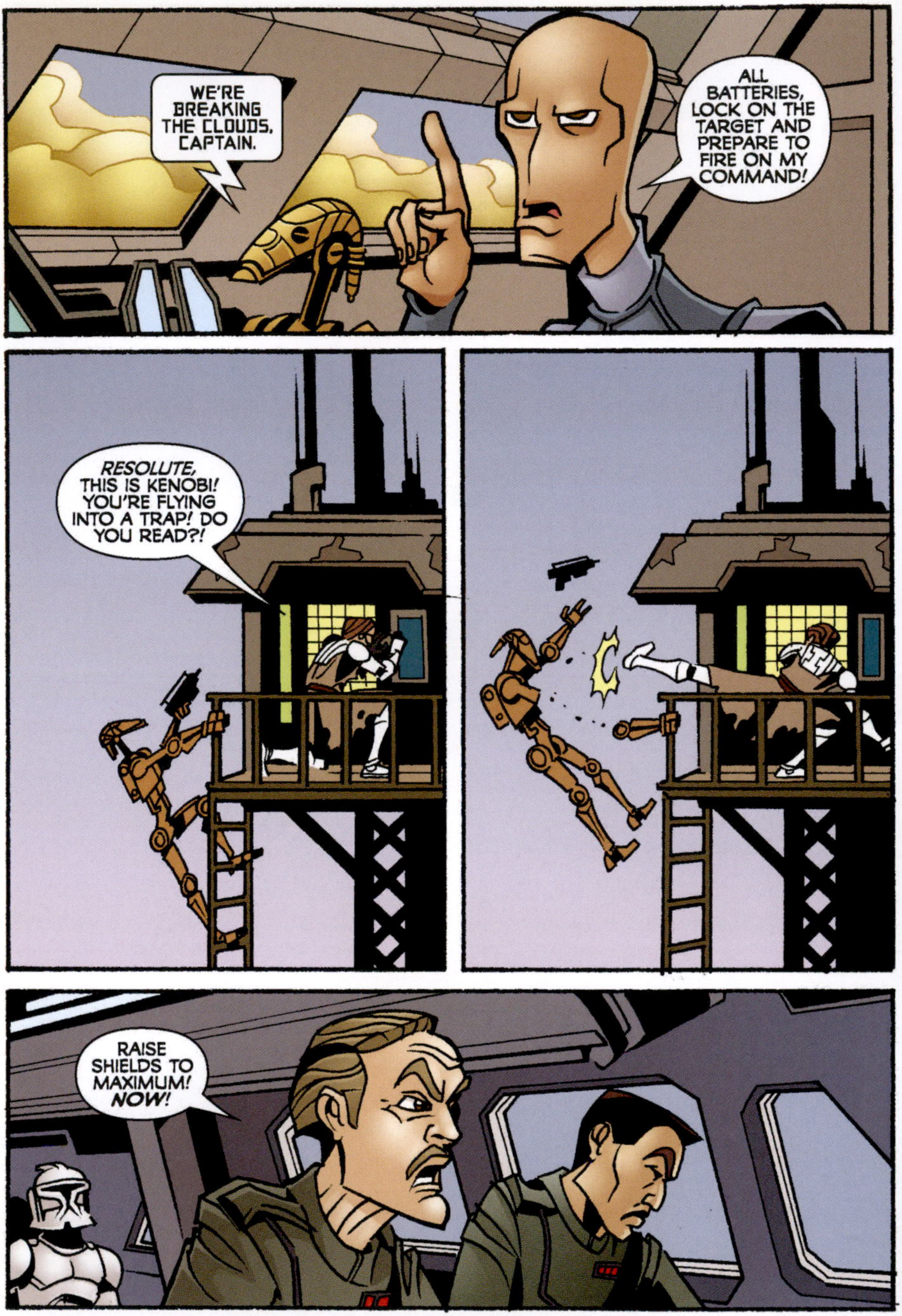
WE'RE BREAKING THE CLOUDS, CAPTAIN.
ALL BATTERIES, LOCK ON THE TARGET AND PREPARE TO FIRE ON MY COMMAND!
RESOLUTE, THIS IS KENOBI! YOU'RE FLYING INTO A TRAP! DO YOU READ?!
RAISE SHIELDS TO MAXIMUM! ***NOW!***

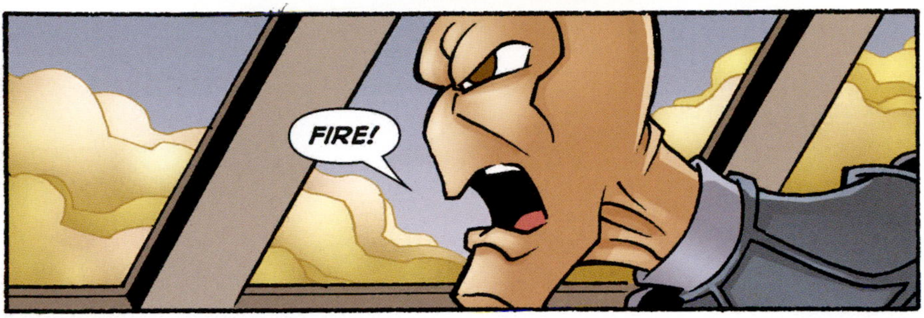
FIRE!

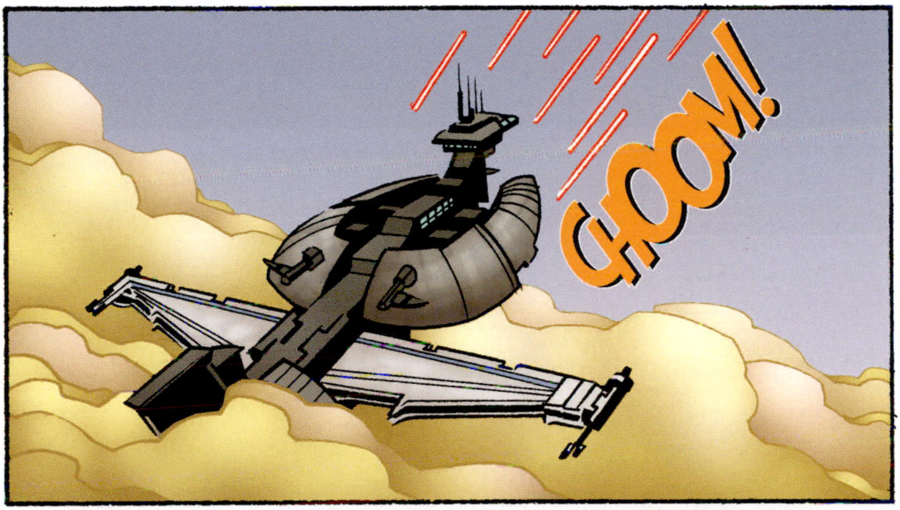
CHOOM!

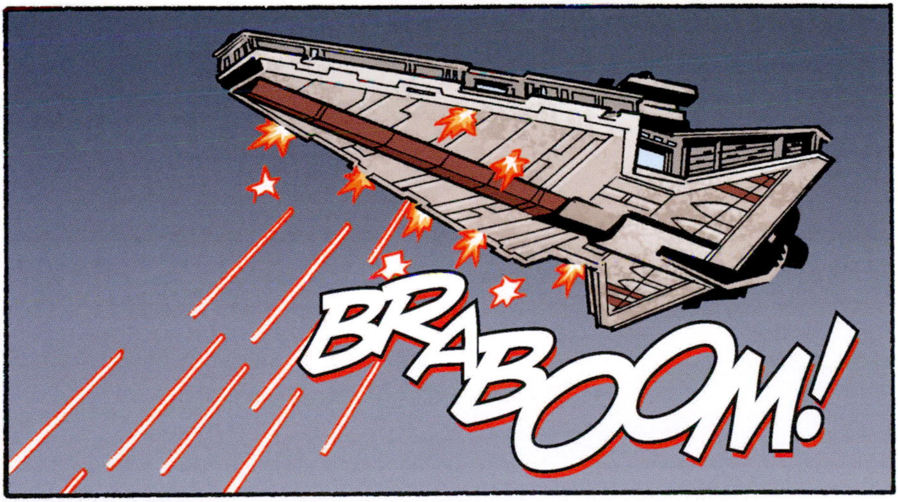
BRABOOM!

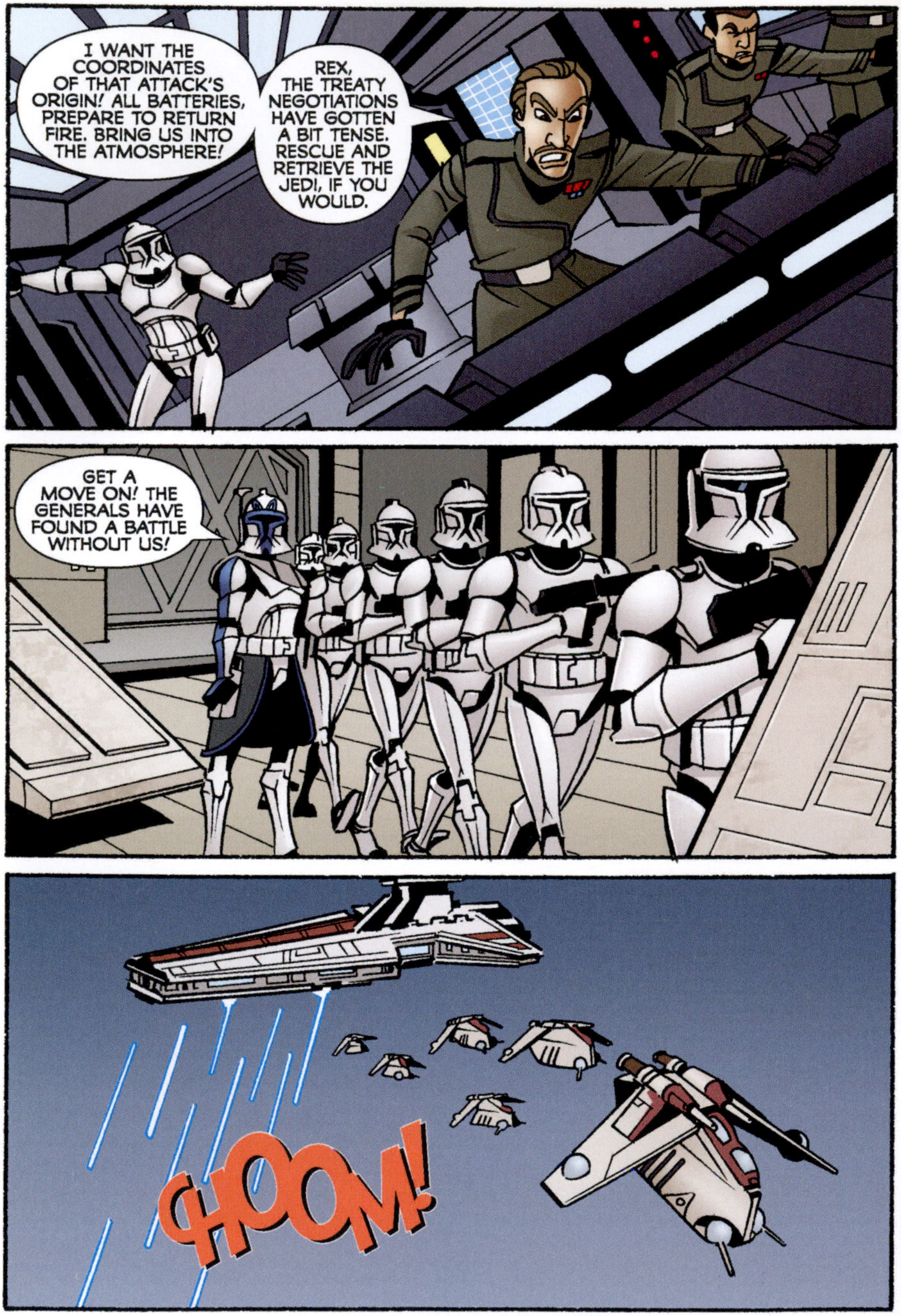
I WANT THE COORDINATES OF THAT ATTACK'S ORIGIN! ALL BATTERIES, PREPARE TO RETURN FIRE. BRING US INTO THE ATMOSPHERE!
REX, THE TREATY NEGOTIATIONS HAVE GOTTEN A BIT TENSE. RESCUE AND RETRIEVE THE JEDI, IF YOU WOULD.
GET A MOVE ON! THE GENERALS HAVE FOUND A BATTLE WITHOUT US!
CHOOM!

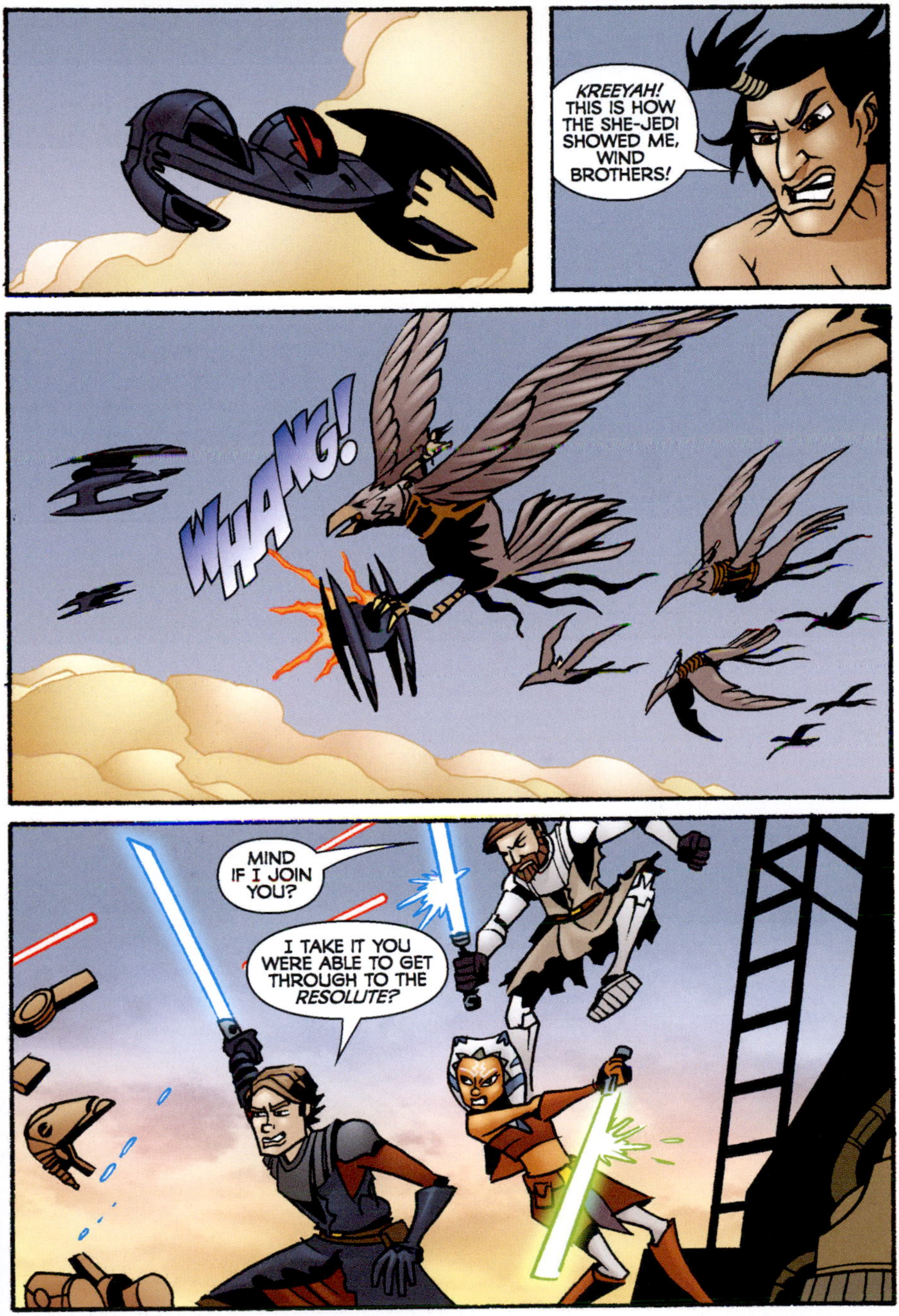

KREEYAH! THIS IS HOW THE SHE-JEDI SHOWED ME, WIND BROTHERS!
WHANG!
MIND IF I JOIN YOU?
I TAKE IT YOU WERE ABLE TO GET THROUGH TO THE RESOLUTE?

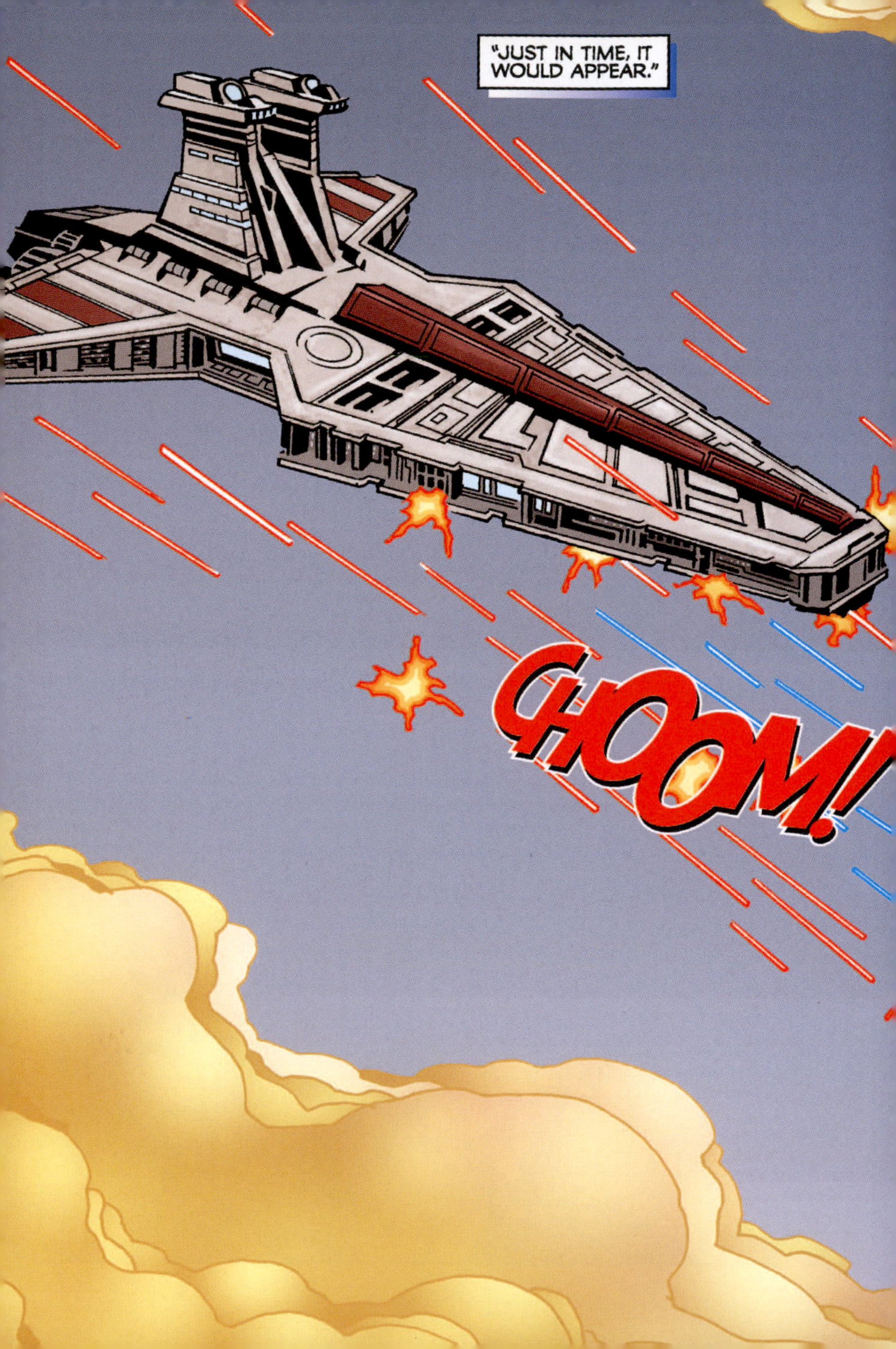
"JUST IN TIME, IT WOULD APPEAR."
CHOOM!

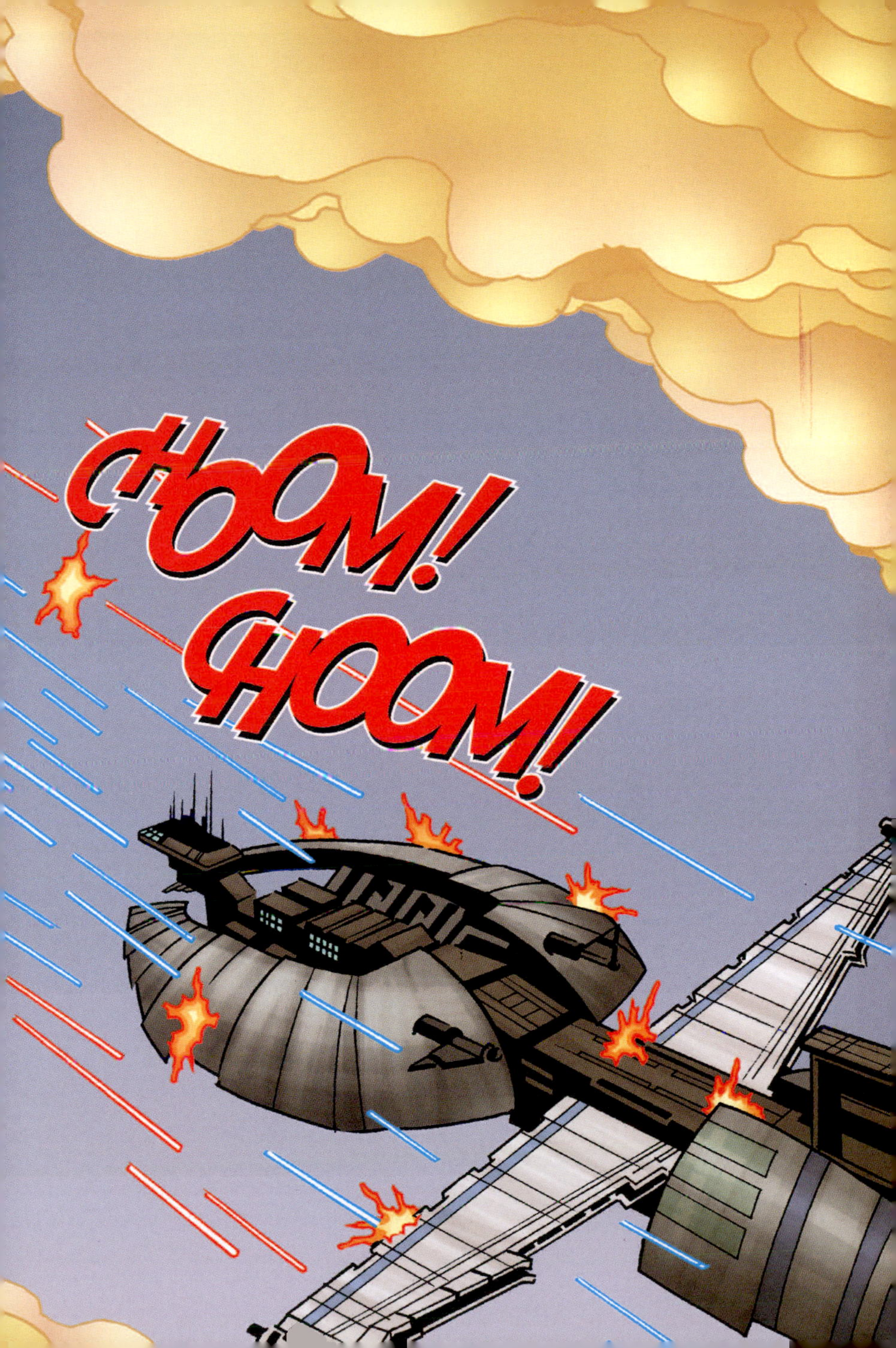
CHOOM!
CHOOM!

THEIR AFT SHIELDS ARE WEAKENING! ALL BATTERIES, TARGET THEIR ENGINES!

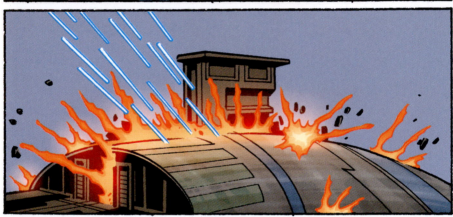

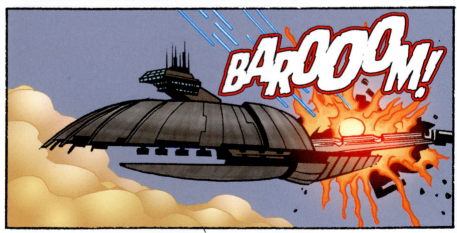

BAROOOM!

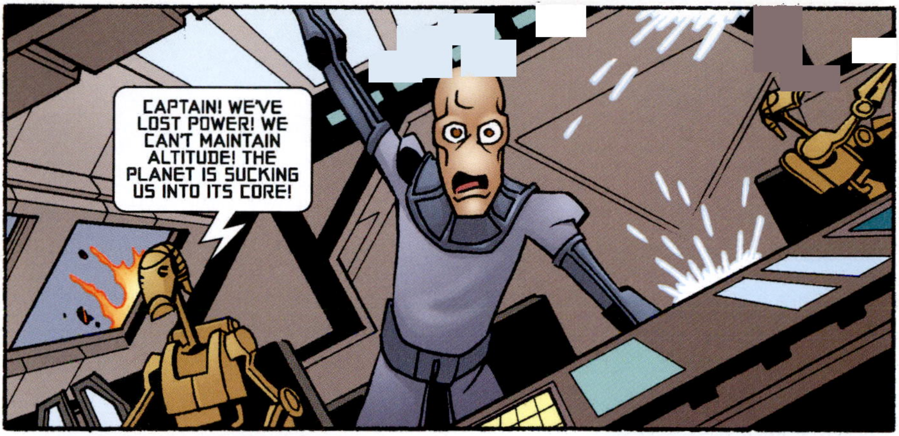
CAPTAIN! WE'VE LOST POWER! WE CAN'T MAINTAIN ALTITUDE! THE PLANET IS SUCKING US INTO ITS CORE!

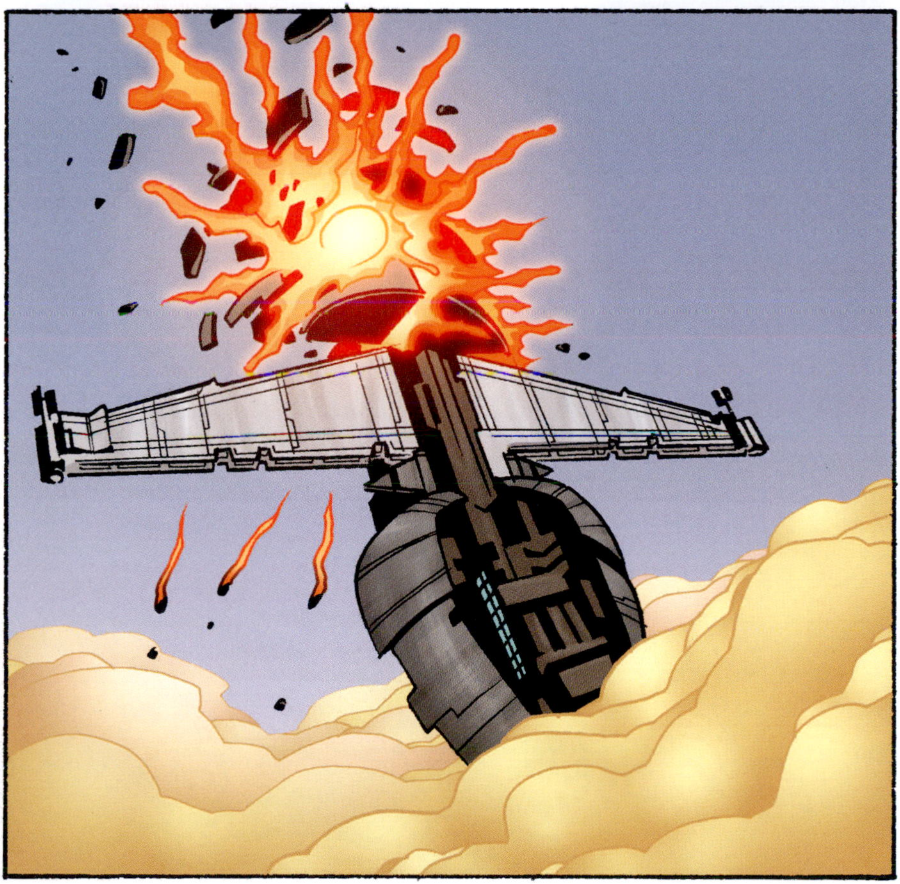

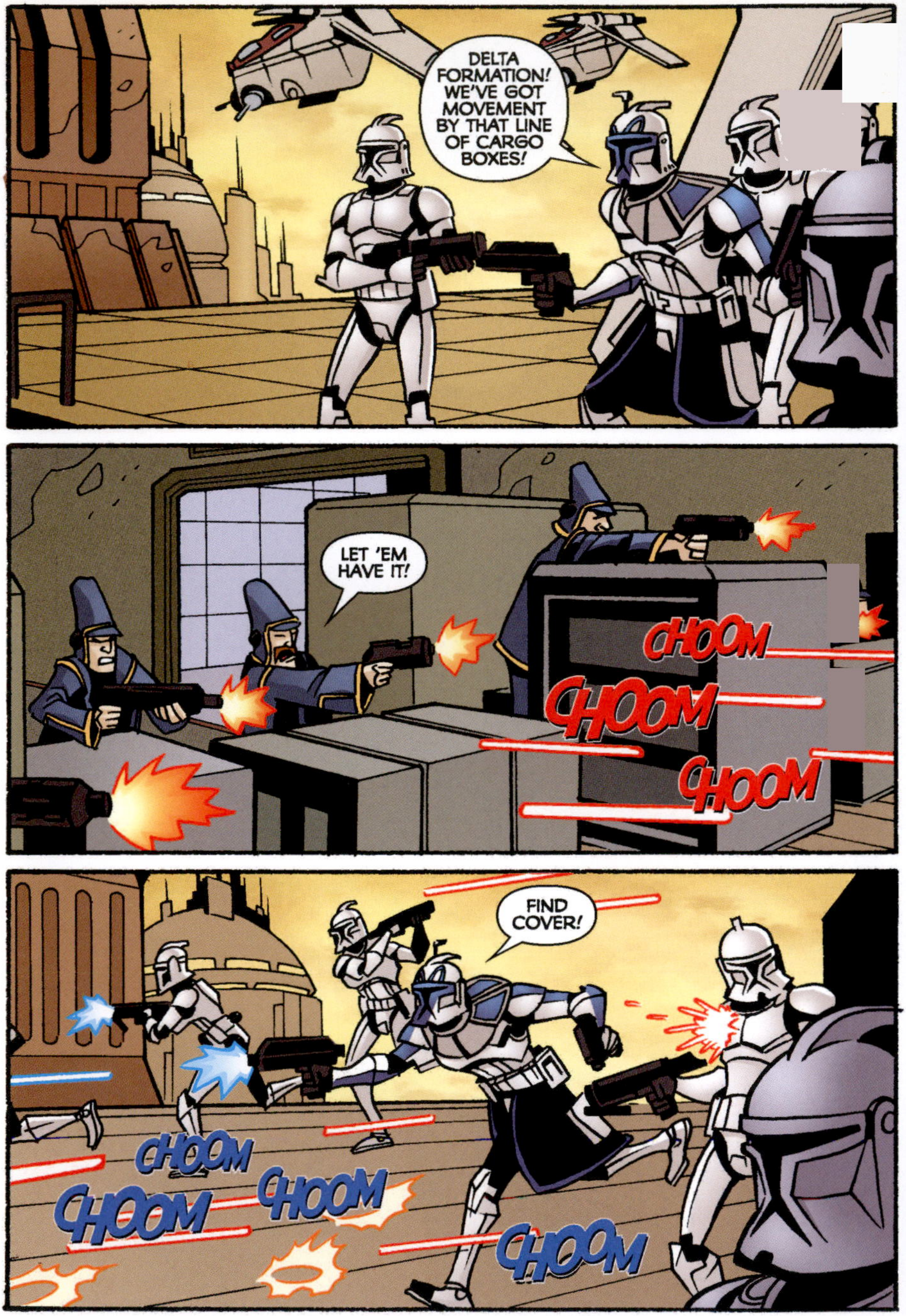
DELTA FORMATION! WE'VE GOT MOVEMENT BY THAT LINE OF CARGO BOXES!
LET 'EM HAVE IT!
CHOOM
CHOOM
CHOOM
FIND COVER!
CHOOM
CHOOM
CHOOM
CHOOM

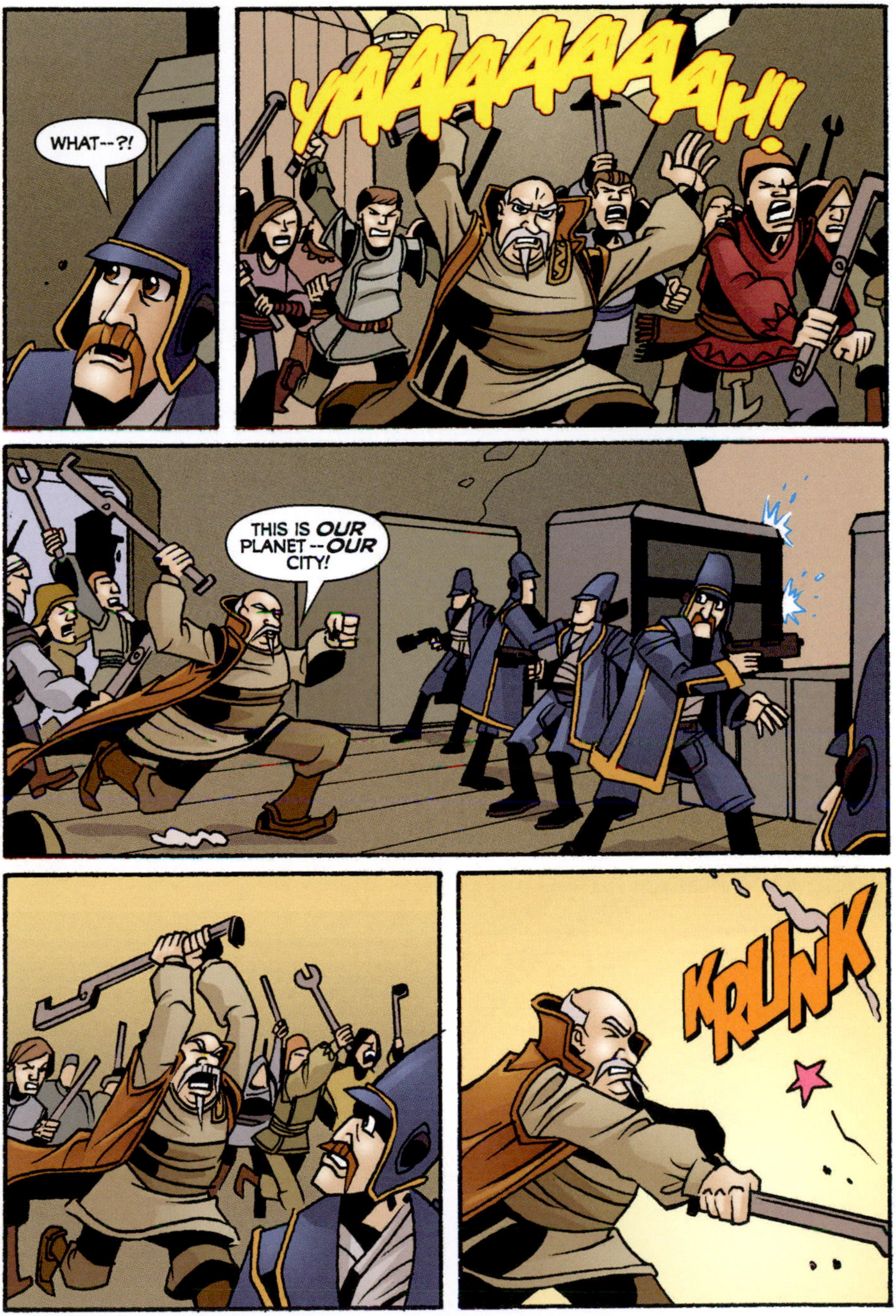
WHAT--?!
YAAAAAAAAAH!
THIS IS OUR PLANET--OUR CITY!
KRUNK

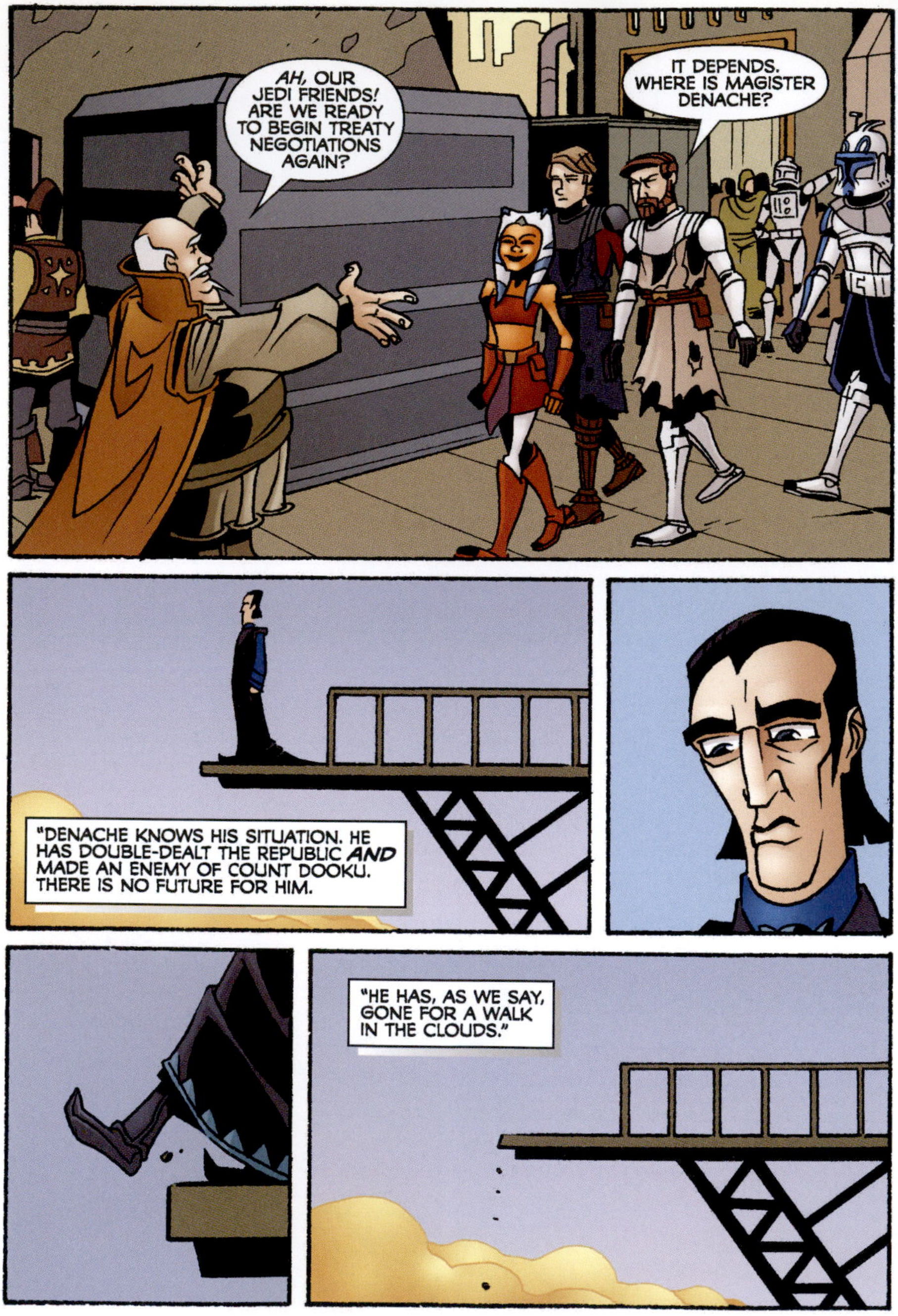
AH, OUR JEDI FRIENDS! ARE WE READY TO BEGIN TREATY NEGOTIATIONS AGAIN?
IT DEPENDS. WHERE IS MAGISTER DENACHE?
"DENACHE KNOWS HIS SITUATION. HE HAS DOUBLE-DEALT THE REPUBLIC AND MADE AN ENEMY OF COUNT DOOKU. THERE IS NO FUTURE FOR HIM.
"HE HAS, AS WE SAY, GONE FOR A WALK IN THE CLOUDS."

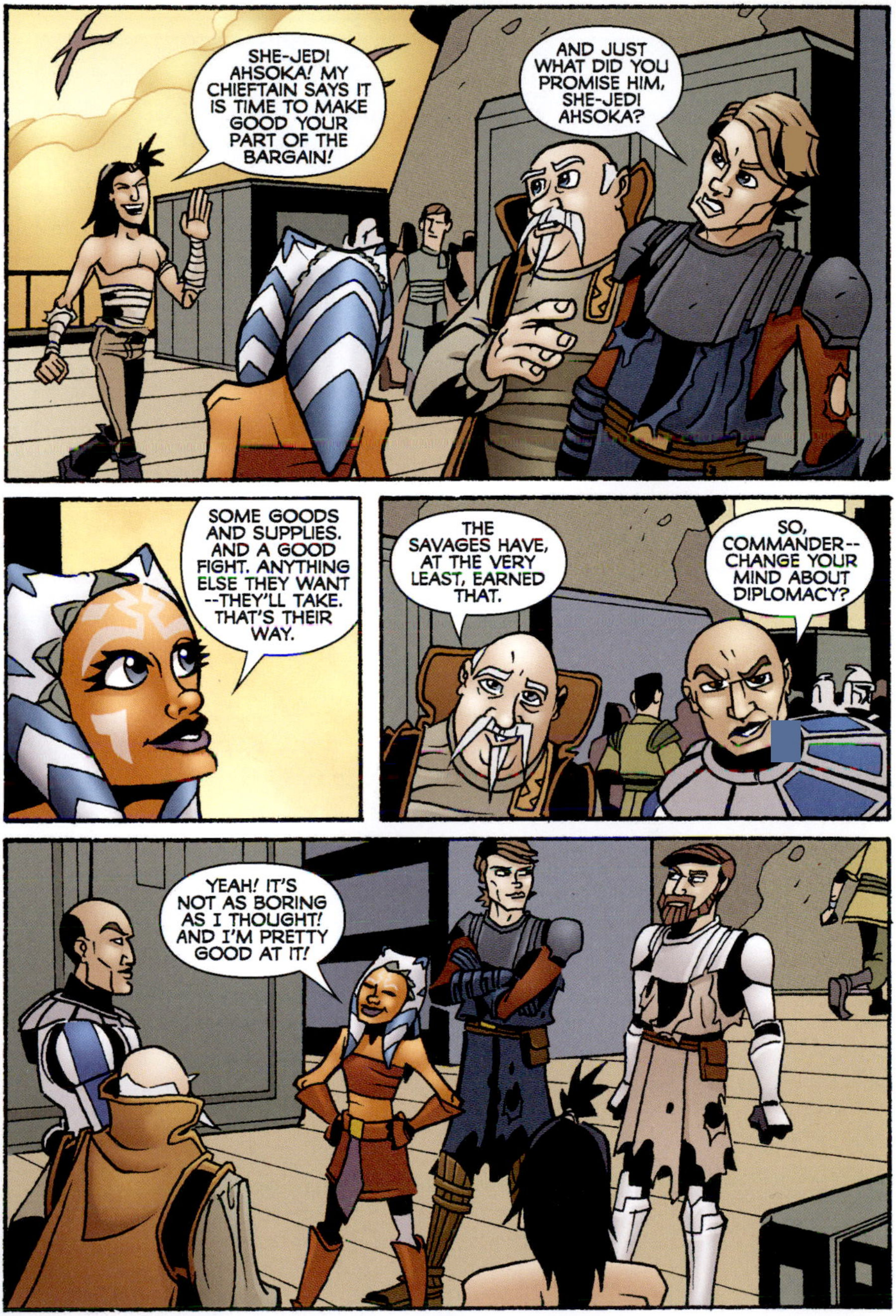
SHE-JEDI AHSOKA! MY CHIEFTAIN SAYS IT IS TIME TO MAKE GOOD YOUR PART OF THE BARGAIN!
AND JUST WHAT DID YOU PROMISE HIM, SHE-JEDI AHSOKA?
SOME GOODS AND SUPPLIES. AND A GOOD FIGHT. ANYTHING ELSE THEY WANT --THEY'LL TAKE. THAT'S THEIR WAY.
THE SAVAGES HAVE, AT THE VERY LEAST, EARNED THAT.
SO, COMMANDER-- CHANGE YOUR MIND ABOUT DIPLOMACY?
YEAH! IT'S NOT AS BORING AS I THOUGHT! AND I'M PRETTY GOOD AT IT!

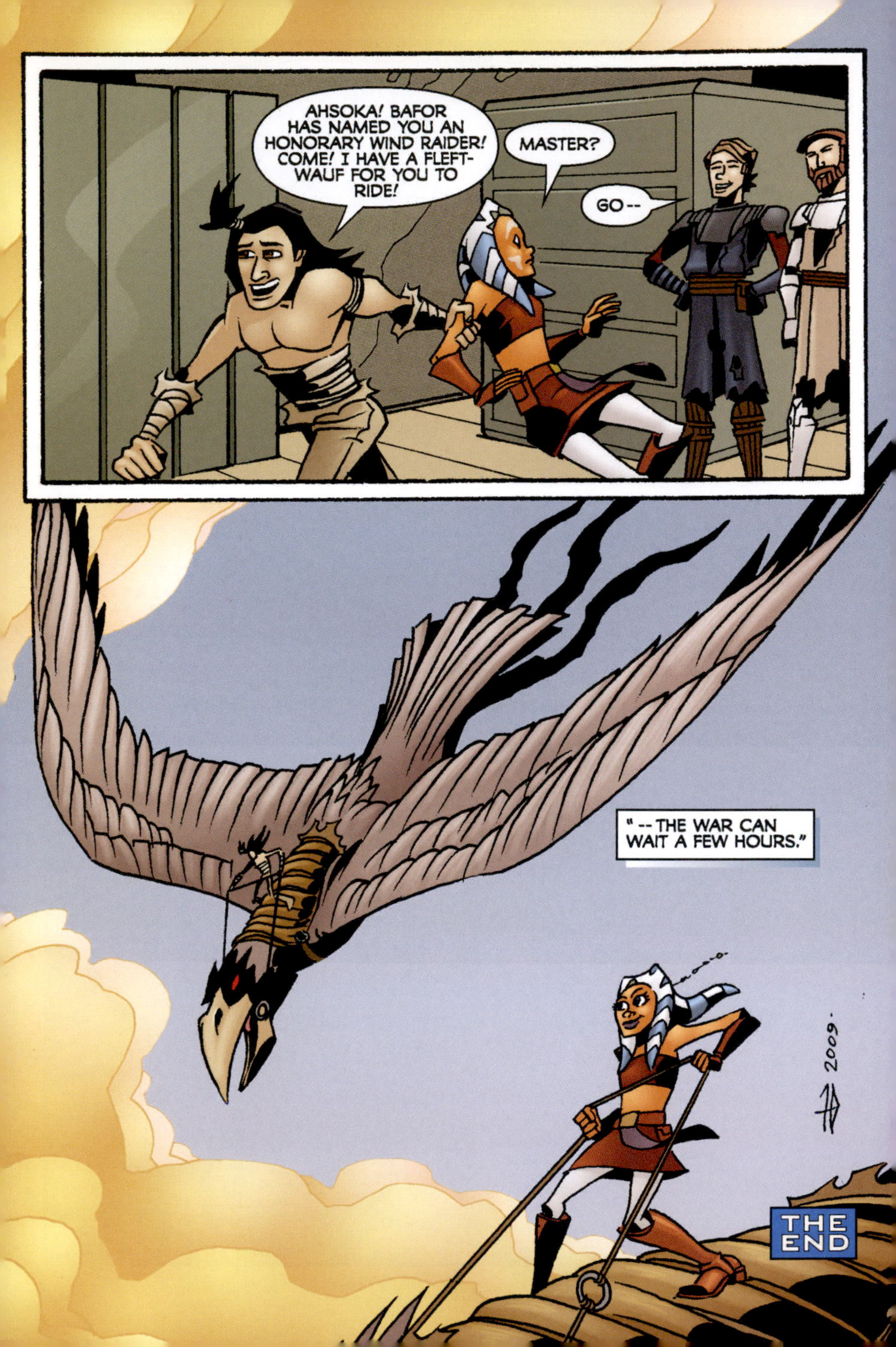
AHSOKA! BAFOR HAS NAMED YOU AN HONORARY WIND RAIDER! COME! I HAVE A FLEFT-WAUF FOR YOU TO RIDE!
MASTER?
GO--
"--THE WAR CAN WAIT A FEW HOURS."
2009
THE END

ALSO AVAILABLE NOW:

STAR WARS
THE CLONE WARS™

CRASH COURSE

N: 9781848562004

STAR WARS
THE CLONE WARS™

SHIPYARDS OF DOOM

ISBN: 9781848561304

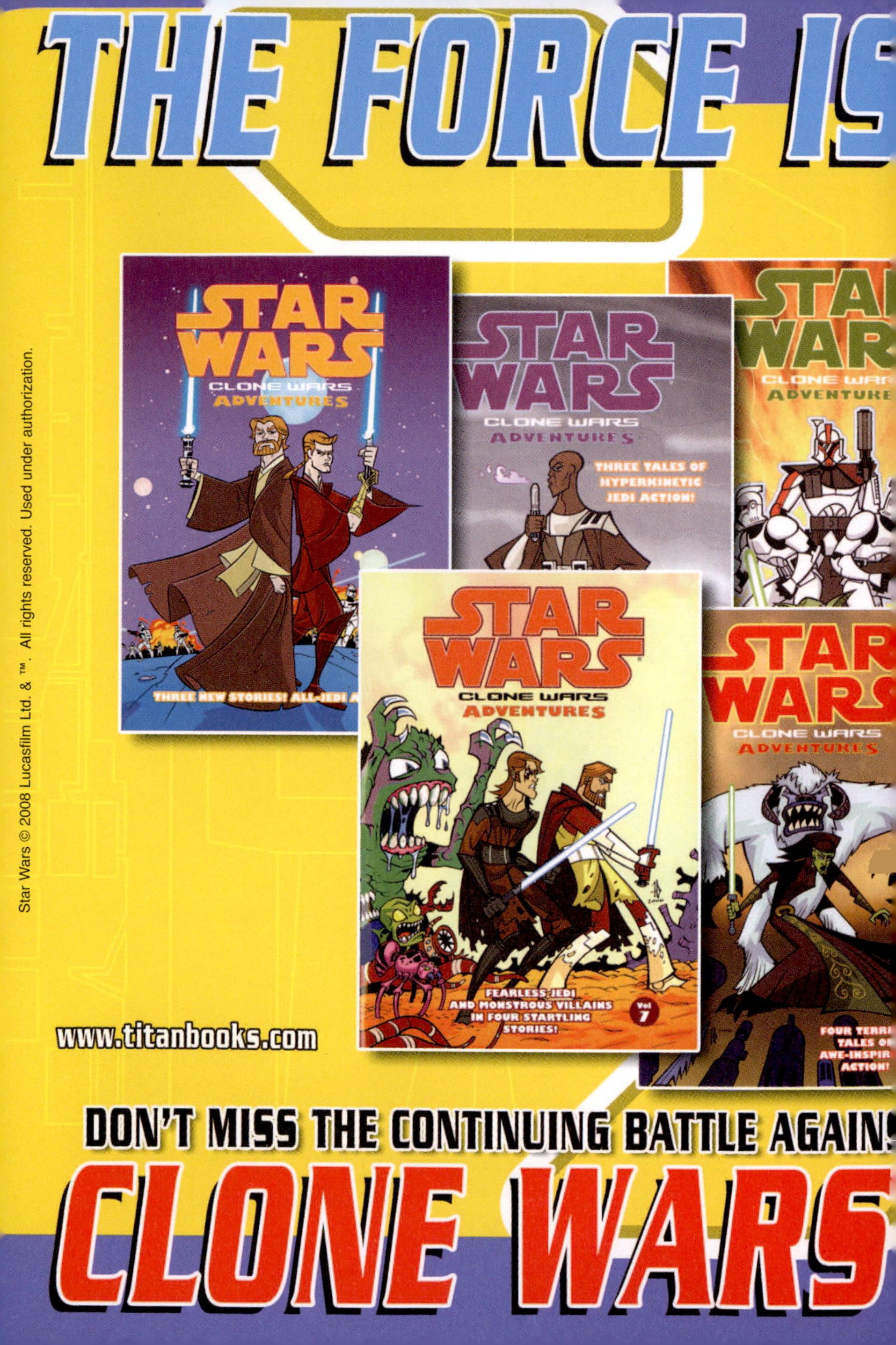
THE FORCE IS
STAR WARS
CLONE WARS
ADVENTURES
THREE TALES OF HYPERKINETIC JEDI ACTION!
FEARLESS JEDI AND MONSTROUS VILLAINS IN FOUR STARTLING STORIES!
Vol 7
www.titanbooks.com
DON'T MISS THE CONTINUING BATTLE AGAIN
CLONE WARS
Star Wars © 2008 Lucasfilm Ltd. & ™. All rights reserved. Used under authorization.

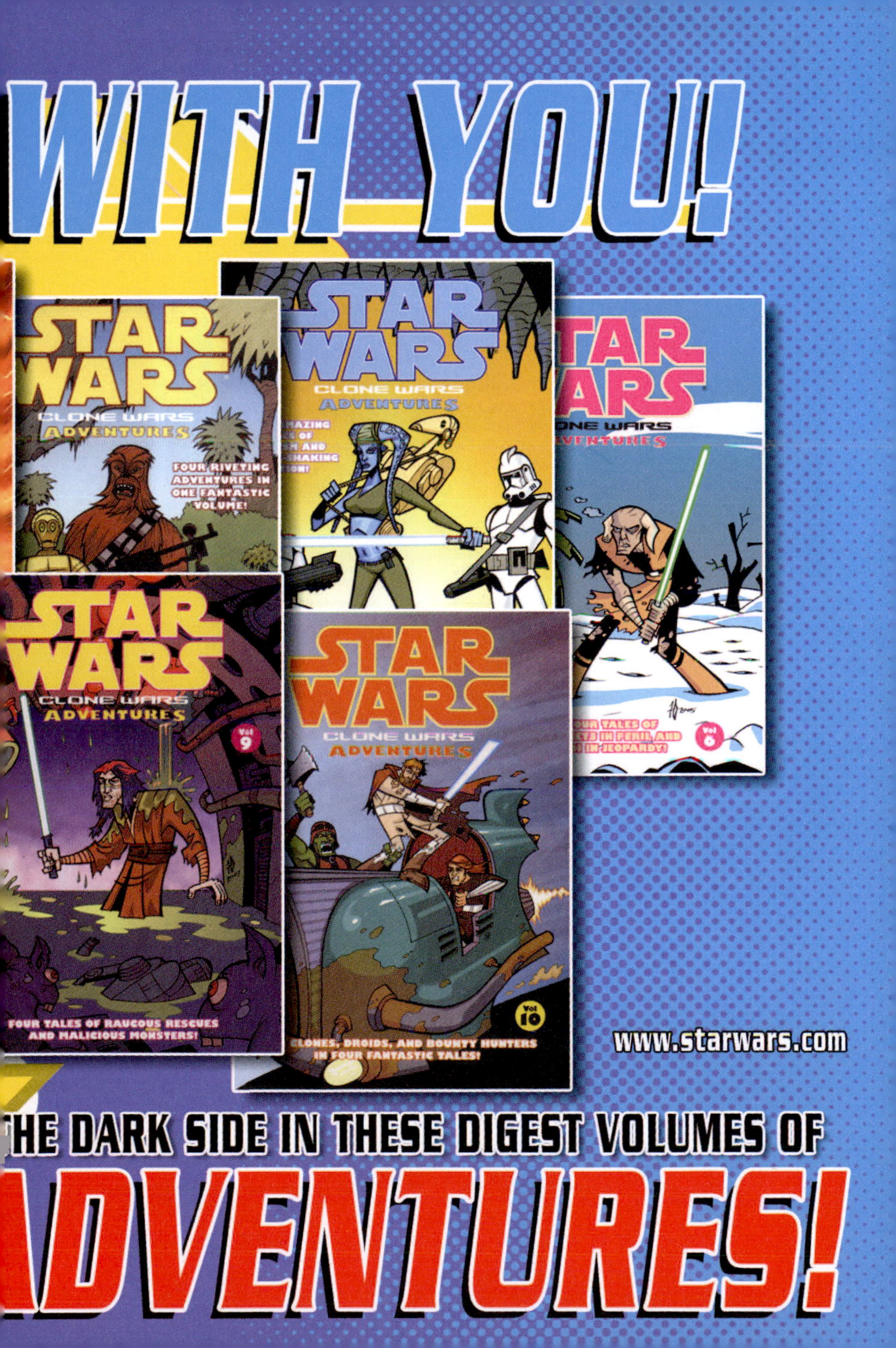

WITH YOU!
STAR WARS
CLONE WARS
ADVENTURES
FOUR RIVETING ADVENTURES IN ONE FANTASTIC VOLUME!
STAR WARS
CLONE WARS
ADVENTURES
STAR WARS
CLONE WARS
ADVENTURES
STAR WARS
CLONE WARS
ADVENTURES
Vol 9
FOUR TALES OF RAUCOUS RESCUES AND MALICIOUS MONSTERS!
STAR WARS
CLONE WARS
ADVENTURES
Vol 10
CLONES, DROIDS, AND BOUNTY HUNTERS IN FOUR FANTASTIC TALES!
www.starwars.com
HE DARK SIDE IN THESE DIGEST VOLUMES OF
DVENTURES!

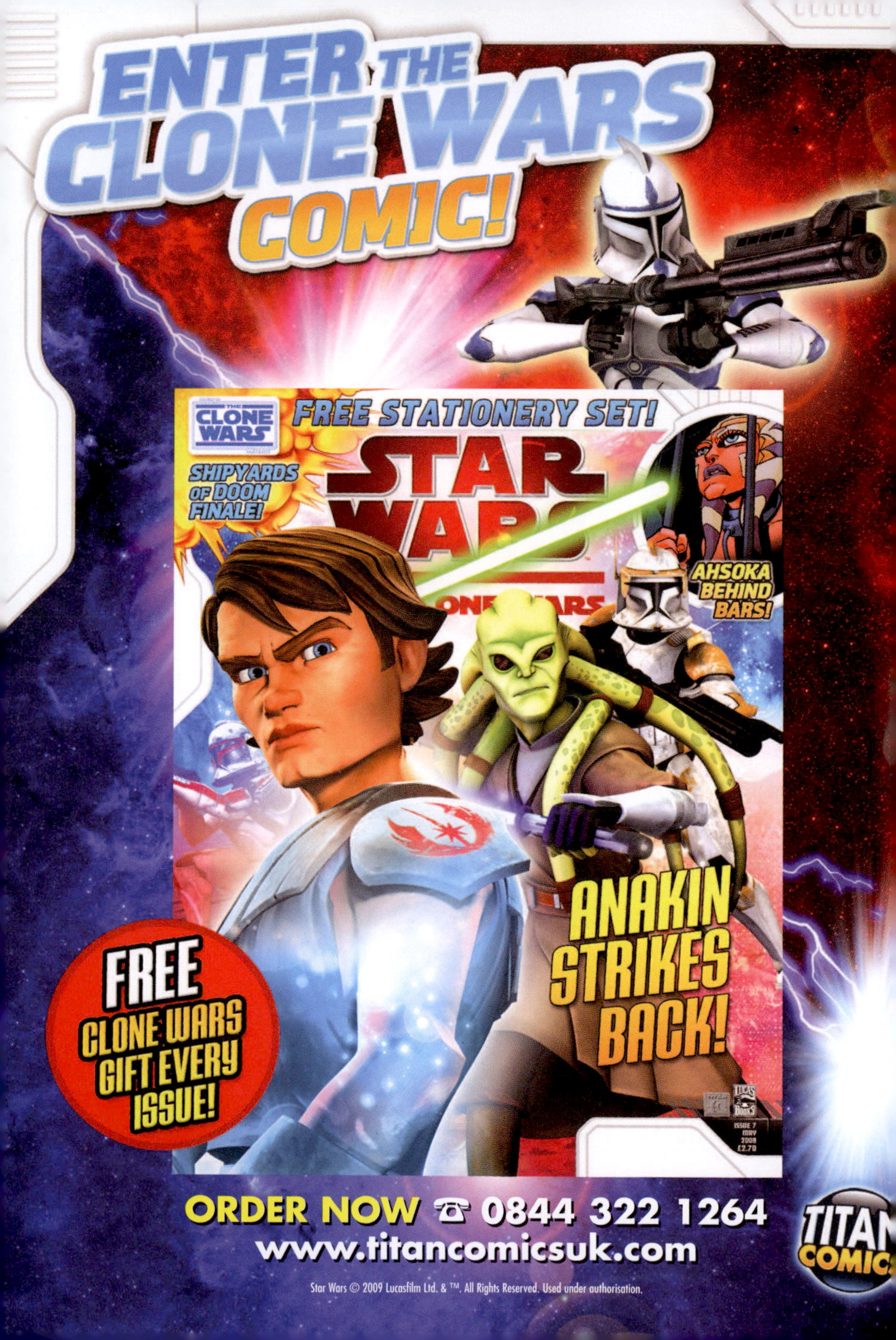

ENTER THE CLONE WARS COMIC!
FREE STATIONERY SET!
THE CLONE WARS
STAR WARS
SHIPYARDS OF DOOM FINALE!
AHSOKA BEHIND BARS!
ANAKIN STRIKES BACK!
FREE CLONE WARS GIFT EVERY ISSUE!
ORDER NOW ☎ 0844 322 1264
www.titancomicsuk.com
TITAN COMICS
Star Wars © 2009 Lucasfilm Ltd. & ™. All Rights Reserved. Used under authorisation.